UNIVERSITY OF NORTH CAROLINA AT CHAPEL HILL

DEPARTMENT OF ROMANCE LANGUAGES

NORTH CAROLINA STUDIES
IN THE ROMANCE LANGUAGES AND LITERATURES

Founder: URBAN TIGNER HOLMES

Distributed by:

UNIVERSITY OF NORTH CAROLINA PRESS
CHAPEL HILL
North Carolina 27514
U.S.A.

NORTH CAROLINA STUDIES IN THE
ROMANCE LANGUAGES AND LITERATURES
Number 188

LANGUAGE IN GIOVANNI VERGA'S
EARLY NOVELS

LANGUAGE IN GIOVANNI VERGA'S EARLY NOVELS

BY

NICHOLAS PATRUNO

CHAPEL HILL

NORTH CAROLINA STUDIES IN THE ROMANCE
LANGUAGES AND LITERATURES
U.N.C. DEPARTMENT OF ROMANCE LANGUAGES

1977

Library of Congress Cataloging in Publication Data

Patruno, Nicholas.
Language in Giovanni Verga's early novels.

(North Carolina studies in the Romance languages and literatures;
no. ~~129~~) 188
Bibliography: p.
1. Verga, Giovanni, 1840-1922 — Language. I. Title. II. Series.

PQ4734.V5Z855   853'.8   77-4731
ISBN 0-8078-9188-6

I.S.B.N. 0-8078-9188-6

IMPRESO EN ESPAÑA
PRINTED IN SPAIN

DEPÓSITO LEGAL: v. 1.917 - 1977   I.S.B.N. 84-399-6618-0
ARTES GRÁFICAS SOLER, S. A. - JÁVEA, 28 - VALENCIA (8) - 1977

PREFACE

The purpose of this study is to examine, analyze and determine the linguistic norm of the early works of Giovanni Verga, namely *Una peccatrice, Storia di una capinera, Eva, Tigre reale* and *Eros.* These works constitute the main body of Verga's so-called "Florentine period," 1866-1875. [1]

Relatively little attention had been given, up until recently, to these early works. As often happens, the mature and best works of an author tend to overshadow his earlier and relatively less important ones. This has certainly been true in the case of Verga. Whereas innumerable books and articles have been written in the last fifty years or so on Verga and on his masterpieces of the "veristic" movement, his earlier works have gone almost unnoticed. Today the situation has changed somewhat since many capable critics — Scaramucci, Musumarra, Luperini, Cecchetti, Sinicropi and Biasin, [2] just to mention a few — have deemed it necessary and useful to give a closer and more detailed look at the early works with the hope of uncovering certain aspects and themes that would

---

[1] Two editions have been used for this study: G. Verga, *Una peccatrice, Storia di una capinera, Eva, Tigre reale,* BMM, 3rd ed. (Milano: 1965) and G. Verga, *Eros,* BMM, 2nd ed. (Milano, 1965). Since there are many citations from the text of the novels, the page number is given in parentheses without the abbreviation "p." in quotations from the first of these two volumes, while quotations from *Eros* are indicated by the page number preceded by "E." unless the title is quoted in the text.

[2] See, e.g., I. Scaramucci, *Introduzione a Verga* (Brescia, 1959); C. Musumarra, *Verga minore* (Pisa, 1965); G. Cecchetti, *"Eros,"* Forum italicum, V-2 (1971), 169-179; G. Sinicropi, "La natura nelle opere di G. V.," *Italica,* XXXVII-2 (1960), 89-108; G. P. Biasin, "Il veleno di Narcisa," *MLN, The Italian Issue,* 85, No. 1 (Jan. 1970), 24-41.

contribute to the sharper delineation of Verga's total literary parabola.

But this long overdue revival of interest in the early works does not yet include, in our opinion, the linguistic dimension. While many of the linguistic aspects of his mature works have been examined in great detail by various critics — Devoto, Spitzer, Hempel, Raya and Caccia [3] being some of them — and rightly so, since Verga is dealing here with, as Devoto puts it, a structurally innovative language, [4] full critical attention has not been given to the linguistic problems of the early works. There are critics — Russo [5] and Raya, for example — who have focused on the language of the early Verga; however, they have tended to examine that language from the perspective of its eventual transcendence by the language of the later, mature period, rather than as an autonomous area. Such an approach necessarily viewed that language in implicitly negative terms, and much of its inherent significance has thereby been left unnoticed.

The existence of this situation has encouraged us to undertake this study, namely, to examine the language of Verga's early period primarily in itself, with the hope that it will aid future research into Verga to view the language of his two periods as an object of comparison, rather than as an example of teleology.

The author thanks the Faculty Awards Committee of Bryn Mawr College for their assistance in making the publication of this study possible. His thanks also go to Professors G. Sinicropi, W. King, S. T. Lachs and to Vito Trimarco for their help and encouragement.

---

[3] See G. Devoto, "Giovanni Verga e i 'Piani del racconto'," *Bollettino del Centro di studi filologici e linguistici siciliani,* II (1954), 271-279 and later also in *Nuovi studi di stilistica* (Firenze, 1962); L. Spitzer, "L'originalità della narrazione nei *Malavoglia*," *Belfagor,* XI (Gennaio 1956), 37-53, W. Hempel, *Giovanni Vargas Roman "I Malavoglia" un die Wiederholung als erzählerisches Kunstmittel* (Koln Graz, Bohlan: Verlag, 1959); G. Raya, *La lingua di Verga* (Firenze, 1962) and E. Caccia, "Il linguaggio dei *Malavoglia* tra storia e poesia," in *Tecniche e valori dal Manzoni al Verga* (Firenze, 1969), pp. 228-265.

[4] G. Devoto and M. L. Altieri, *La lingua italiana, storia e problemi attuali* (Torino, 1968), p. 121; see also G. Devoto, *Profilo di storia linguistica italiana,* 4th ed. (Firenze, 1966), p. 154 esp.

[5] The chapter "La lingua di Verga" appeared for the first time in Russo's 3rd revised and amplified edition of *Giovanni Verga* (Napoli-Milano, 1941). We have availed ourselves, however, of the "Universale Laterza" (Bari, 1966) edition.

TABLE OF CONTENTS

INTRODUCTION: AN HISTORICAL PERSPECTIVE

When Giovanni Verga went to Florence in 1865, Italy, in the aftermath of the Unification, was still faced with problems of various sorts and among these the "questione della lingua" had gained major importance. A problem that existed, primarily on a literary level, from Dante's time had now become more alive and more pertinent than ever: because of the ever growing national sentiment, it assumed, paradoxically, larger and more polemic proportions. The country, with the rate of illiteracy almost as high as 80 %,[1] was faced with a perplexing situation: if, on the one hand, it recognized that a unified language was the best, if not the only, social instrument to represent a nation that was politically and spiritually united,[2] it was also true, on the other hand, that the customs and nature of the various Italian regions, perhaps still very much embedded in their own past traditions, made it difficult to bring such a needed reform.[3] The fact that dialects were still very much in predominance proved the heterogeneity of the local customs and at the same time reflected the "ristagno plurisecolare,"[4] on the economic, social and intellectual levels, of the country's past ages. Ascoli was correct in noting that Italy lacked the centripetal forces[5] needed for the desired Unification. Industrialization and urbanization for example, important contributing forces for the concretion of a national unity — and a common language — were only at their

---

[1] Tullio De Mauro, *Storia linguistica dell'Italia unita*, U.L. (Bari, 1965), p. 32.

[2] Bruno Migliorini, *Storia della lingua italiana*, 2nd ed. (Firenze, 1960), p 590.

[3] De Mauro, p. 17 especially.

[4] *Ibid.*, p. 19.

[5] Cf. his "Proemio," *Archivio Glottologico Italiano*, I (1873).

beginning and too weak therefore to exert much influence. As a result of this amorphous situation, the Italian language, even though "amata e celebrata"[6] by most, was for the most part restricted to the expression of political and cultural phenomena, for most of the people refrained from using it in everyday matters since they found it, for one reason or another, alien to them. It was no wonder therefore that in a nation where the so-called "Italian" language was practiced by such a small social minority — in addition to those that had received a formal education, only those dialects used in and around Florence came closest to the generally accepted language — it would have been a very difficult task to agree upon a form of expression acceptable to the entire populace.

There were many men who offered suggestions as to which regional norm to adopt. Some preferred one dialect to another, others were for the combining of the different dialects and there were those interested in adopting what had been up to then the literary Italian language, namely the Florentine. To the first group belonged, for example, Agatino Longo who, in the introduction to a collection of Sicilian proverbs, presented a theory on the validity of the Sicilian dialect as a national language.[7] Much more interest, however, was aroused by the theories and suggested programs of Manzoni and G. I. Ascoli.

After his trip to Florence, in 1827, which must have been, as Migliorini points out, somewhat of a "rivelazione,"[8] Manzoni, partly influenced by the cultured Florentines he had met, felt that he had finally found a language that was "viva, agile e reale."[9] Because of this, as a writer of the Romantic movement and as a citizen keenly aware of the need for a linguistic reform, he suggested that the Florentine be adopted. Feeling that "ciò che costituisce una lingua non è l'appartenere a un'estensione maggiore o minore di paese, ma l'essere una quantità di vocaboli adeguata agli usi di una società effettivamente vera,"[10] he saw in the Florentine the language

---

[6] De Mauro, p. 17.

[7] "Proverbi e modi di dire siciliani illustrati dal cav. Agatino Longo," *Borghini*, II (1864), 375-76.

[8] *Storia*, p. 611.

[9] *Ibid.*, p. 612.

[10] In his letter to Giacinto Carena: in *Scritti linguistici*, ed. F. Barbieri (Torino, 1924), p. 12.

that best suited the new form of society. His choice of the language was not only a question of change in his personal style but, more importantly, a way of reforming and reshaping the language as a social institution. He also had a paradigmatic aim in mind. Sensing that society could no longer effectively function within the limitations of the language as it was, he wanted to get rid of out-moded forms and replace them with more relevant ones and hoped that he, as a writer, would be able to contribute to such changes. [11] What Manzoni successfully did do, in other words, was to make of language no longer an issue that concerned only, as it had up to then, men of letters but a civil problem that involved and affected the entire nation. He was hoping that political unification could bring about, through an organized educational system that would act equally throughout Italy and on all social levels, the institution of a Florentine-based language. But, as he failed to see, his plan could have taken effect only if there were "profonde trasformazioni della mentalità dominante," [12] something very unlikely to occur without adequate and drastic changes in the social structure of Italy. Regardless of this, however, the much revered Manzoni, whose literary influence had already been felt and esteemed for some time, found that his theory was favorably received especially by some of his fellow writers and political figures.

Even if Manzoni failed to see the nation's intricate social problems, he still maintained that the most logical step would be to adopt Florentine since it was, among the many norms, the one that was best known to more people. Tommaseo, who was also concerned with the linguistic problem, seemed best to express what Manzoni might have had in mind. Looking at the situation from a practical point of view, he bluntly stated that "il toscano è da presciegliere, per la ragione assai valida, ch'e' fu sempre, a dispetto de' litiganti, e dai più savi de' litiganti stessi, prescelto.... Egli (the Tuscan) era da prescegliere perchè più gentile." [13] Manzoni also

---

[11] See Migliorini's "La questione della lingua," in *Questioni e correnti di storia letteraria* (Milano, 1965), p. 57.

[12] De Mauro, p. 41.

[13] *Dizionario dei sinonimi*, rev. 5th ed. (Napoli, 1866), p. 15. In the preface of this book, in p. 16, Tommaseo goes on to say that the Tuscan was to be used because it was the only language that had the three basic norms that determined its beauty: the most significant "etimologia," "l'analogia filosofica e grammaticale" and "l'armonia musicale e l'onomatopeica."

found a very strong ally in Minister Broglio who, taking advantage of his political position, entrusted him with the task of compiling a vocabulary based on the Florentine language.

Manzoni's most articulate opponent on the linguistic issue was G. I. Ascoli who, approaching the linguistic problem with a much more realistic view of Italy's historical situation, saw that the almost forced linguistic indoctrination that Manzoni was suggesting was highly impractical and not congenial to the nation's needs. "Il volere oggi, — he stated — nell'età della riflessione, che si lasci di punto in bianco il modo sempre usato da tutti gl'Italiani, e si turbi la norma etimologica, evidente a tutti e sentita da tutti ... è proprio un fare troppo a fidanza con la bontà degli uomini." [14] Unlike Manzoni, he contended that the true elements of the "lingua viva" were to be found in the various dialects since they, regardless of all the proposed theories and programs, were and had been historically the only common denominator of the nation's intellectual endeavor. The national language had to be based therefore on "l'idioma vivo di un dato municipio, che per questo capo viene a farsi principe, o quasi stromento livellatore, dell'intiera nazione." [15] With this statement he showed himself to be in complete disagreement with Manzoni's belief that a language "non è, se non è un tutto ; e a volerla prendere un po' di qua e un po' di là, è il modo d'immaginarsi perpetuamente di farla, senza averla fatta mai." [16] Resorting once again to history, Ascoli pointed out that Italy, because of her economic and social structures, could not nor should be compared to other nations, and to Germany and France in particular. If Paris served as the emanating linguistic center of France it wasn't necessarily true that Florence, contrary to Manzoni's view, could have the same function in Italy. In fact, he felt that "fiorentinismo," rather than widening "l'attività mentale della nazione," [17] would have exactly the opposite effect. Because of his strong belief in the importance and validity of the dialects, Ascoli founded the famous *Archivio Glottologico,* whose aim was, as he

---

[14] "Proemio," XXIV.

[15] *Ibid.,* IX.

[16] A. Manzoni, "Dell'unità della Lingua e dei mezzi di diffonderla," in *Prose* (Firenze, 1931), II, 126.

[17] Ascoli, "Proemio," XXXII.

stated in its preface, to promote the "esplorazione scientifica" [18] of the Italian dialects still in existence.

Ascoli's views were also shared by other men of prominence. De Sanctis and D'Ovidio, for example, also believed that the intrinsic literary value and tradition of the various dialects were important assets to the enrichment of the national culture. Rather than being forsaken, they should be examined more closely and compared to the accepted language for the purpose of bringing out the existing diversities and preserving at the same time their vital elements.

The linguistic problems were, of course, also very much alive on the more strictly literary level. Migliorini is very clear in tracing the two opposite and prevalent views [19] that were in existence even before the linguistic problem had gained a nationalistic dimension. The purists and classicists who wanted to rid the language of the various barbarisms and impurities were opposed by the writers of "Romanticismo" who, seeking a language that was both "viva e vera," were inspired by the spoken language. This group, led and stirred primarily by Manzoni, wanted a language that was the product of the entire society and that would best reflect all of its needs. Believing, in other words, that literature had a social commitment, they felt that the language used ought to be one understood by all.

Opposite to these views and echoing from a distance the voices of Leopardi and Foscolo was Carducci who, looking at the "questione della lingua" mainly from the vantage point of style and art, stressed that the only language fit for literary expression was that based on the works of the authors and poets of past centuries. "Odio — he stated — la lingua accademica . . . ma amo, adoro la lingua di Dante e del Petrarca, la lingua dei poeti popolari del quattrocento, la lingua degli elegantissimi poeti del cinquecento, la lingua dei poeti classici dell'ultima età; amo e studio e uso a tempo la lingua del popolo, la nata e non la fatta lingua del popolo." [20] Without denying the usefulness and aesthetic value of the "nata e non fatta" spoken language, but to be used only when needed, it is clear that Carducci, unlike the "manzoniani," did not believe that literature

---

[18] *Ibid.*, XXXV.
[19] See Migliorini, "Questione," pp. 50-66.
[20] G. Carducci, *Prose* (Bologna, 1924), p. 682.

was meant to be read and appreciated by all. He, for one, attributed much more value to poetry than to prose.

Although the views held by the Romanticists, since they were more responsive to the deep changes that were taking place in social sentiment and in all forms of contemporary literature, [21] were more readily accepted, it should be noted that the conservative minded classicists did play a constructive role in the "questione della lingua." If Manzoni's work, for example, succeeded in extirpating from the literary tradition the very ancient "cancro della retorica," [22] the classicists preserved the essence of such tradition by condemning what they considered all unnecessary exoticisms and neologisms, serving thus as an antidote to the "sciatteria" and "francesismo" [23] that, because of the predominant influence of French culture in Italy, always posed a threat to the integrity of the Italian language.

As a result of the success of the Romantic movement, which in Italy meant the adoption of Manzoni's views, most non-Tuscan writers, desirous of bringing to the same level the written and the spoken language, were faced by two alternatives: either write in a language decisively influenced by their respective regions — i.e. Ippolito Nievo, Rovani — or go to Florence and make their own the essence of what was still held as the best norm for literary expression.

Going to Florence meant not only an improvement in the handling of stylistic skills but also meant entering into an atmosphere that was, in all aspects, very conducive to creative work. With the Unification, as Giovanni Gentile stated, "la Toscana s'era aperta, era divenuta l'Italia; e nella nuova vita nazionale cominciavano ad entrare e circolare più rapidamente le idee e i bisogni spirituali del secolo, attraendo e trascinando gli animi con la forza del nuovo." [24] Even during the years of the Risorgimento, with all its political dissensions and polemics, Florence had been able, as in the past, to remain culturally above the rest of Italy and, enjoying relatively prosperous economic conditions, had managed to keep

---

[21] See Ernesto Masi, *Il Risorgimento italiano* (Firenze, 1917), p. 507.
[22] Ascoli, "Proemio," XXVIII.
[23] Migliorini, *Storia*, p. 592.
[24] *Gino Capponi e la cultura toscana del secolo decimonono* (Firenze, 1926), p. 328.

a generally liberal and tolerant government. The fact, too, that Florence during these years of turmoil had been free of foreign intrusions not only made possible the preservation of her deeply rooted traditions but contributed to making her feel in harmony with the rising new trends of life and with the latest literary experiences, both national and European. "Tutto, in Firenze . . . era accolto e discusso, per così dire, alla giornata, con gusto sperimentale . . . . Si fa sentire con forza la presenza . . . d'una civiltà o di un'unità regionale abbastanza nettamente distinta." [25] Florence's benign and congenial conditions continued to attract, therefore, the most emancipated and creative minds of the time and kept on providing opportunities to artists as well as a safe asylum to political exiles. In short, in this period considered by Grazzini as part of the "centenario della pacifica rivoluzione toscana," [26] Florence continued to be the city chosen by artists and scholars, both Italian and foreign, who were seeking "la visione diretta dei modelli inimitabili e la tranquillità feconda dell'*otium latino*." [27] Men such as La Farina, Capuana, Vannucci, Guerrazzi, Ricasoli and Capponi were able, in Florence, to keep their literary interests alive and to express them not only in discussions but in reviews and comments published in the various Florentine journals.

There is no doubt that Verga too was soon attracted by this city's conditions. When he went to Florence, the city was, in fact, even more active than before since it had just been declared capital of Italy, thus enlarging her already eminent role to encompass also the state's political affairs, and was celebrating Dante's sixth centenary by further expanding her numerous cultural programs. Verga, like the provincial who for the first time goes to the city, was completely overwhelmed and captivated by this city's tempo and cultural wealth. He enjoyed being a witness of the important events and decisions destined to formulate the future of Italy and took comfort in finding himself among those — Dall'Ongaro, Prati, Alear-

---

[25] Aldo Borlenghi, introduction to *Narratori dell'ottocento e del primo novecento* (Milano-Napoli, 1961), I, XXV.

[26] Giovanni Grazzini, Preface to *Il montanino toscano* by Giuseppe Tigri. In the collection "Il Ventriquattesimo," ed. Cecchi and Branca (Firenze, 1959).

[27] Aldo Ferrari, *La preparazione intellettuale del Risorgimento (1748-1789)* (Milano, 1923), p. 108.

di, Maffei, Fusinato and others — who could offer him assistance and encouragement, and appreciate his literary efforts. In 1869 Verga wrote that "Firenze è davvero il centro della vita politica e intellettuale d'Italia; qui si vive in un'altra atmosfera ... e per diventare qualche cosa bisogna vivere al còntatto di queste illustrazioni — farsi riconoscere, e conoscere, respirarne l'aria insomma.... È indispensabile incominciare di qui la propria strada; e non si può fare a meno di riescire a qualche cosa." [28]

Because of the limited literary assistance that his teachers, Domenico Castorina and Antonino Abate, were able to furnish him with and because of the somewhat isolated literary milieu of Sicily, which had tended to keep him away from "la circolazione viva delle idee," [29] Verga in his very first novels clearly revealed himself as a late writer of a predominantly Romantic vein. Although there are indications that, as Luperini points out, he was inspired somewhat by the works of Alfieri and Foscolo, he was influenced mainly by the more popular French writers of the time — i.e. Dumas and Feuillet. His first works received very little attention except, perhaps, for *I carbonari della montagna*, [30] so filled with patriotic ardor that he sent to the politically active Guerrazzi a copy of this novel which received a rather encouraging review from the periodical *La nuova Europa* (May 23, 1862). The reviewer, in addition to noticing the various weak points, praised the young writer for his honest efforts and sensitivity; as for the language, it was "buona in generale ma non troppo pura."

When Verga went to Florence (and here Devoto's observations on Manzoni seen very well suited for our writer too), he presented himself "alla tradizione linguistica italiana dal di fuori, dominandone ... l'aspetto espressivo attraverso la padronanza del dialetto, e quello tecnico sopranazionale attraverso la conoscenza del francese. La sua familiarità con la lingua letteraria era modesta e con-

---

[28] From one of the "Lettere di Giovanni Verga a sua madre," *Fiera Letteraria*, Rome, July 20, 27, Aug. 3, 10, 17, 1930, cited by L. Russo, *Giovanni Verga* (Bari, 1966), p. 37.

[29] Romano Luperini, *Pessimismo e Verismo in Giovanni Verga* (Padova, 1968), p. 22.

[30] This novel, published in four volumes (Catania, 1861-62), was preceded by *Amore e patria*, a novel which was never published, and followed by *Sulle lagune*, which appeared in installments in *Nuova Europa* (Firenze, Jan. 13-March 15, 1863).

venzionale." [31] Well aware of his linguistic limitations, he believed that in this city he would find the tools of expression adequate to his inspiration and for him it was of the utmost necessity and importance to live in a place that could furnish, for the sake of giving life to his works, the accepted colloquialisms and popular expressions. He stated that "il predicato studio del vocabolario è falso, perchè il valore d'uso non vi si può imparare. Ascoltando, ascoltando, si impara a scrivere. E da questo deriva la mia teoria dello stile. Lo stile non esiste fuori dell'idea..." [32] And Tuscan usages such as *le davamo la berta, io sono la tua sorella, baloccarsi* and others to be seen later do testify to his listening and to his intention of remaining within the range of the live language or, to use Terracini's terms, "del linguaggio in atto." [33] Further proof is supplemented by the closeness, in terms of sentence structure and vocabulary, of Verga's prose to that of newspaper reporters. Verga was, in fact, "ascoltando," since newspapers reflected most closely the standard language most likely to be absorbed by a society such as the one being treated by the author. [34] It appears that Verga, in

---

[31] G. Devoto, *Profilo di storia linguistica*, p. 124.
[32] U. Ojetti, *Alla ricerca dei letterati* (Milano, 1895), p. 87.
[33] Benvenuto Terracini, *Analisi stilistica* (Milano, 1966), p. 5.
[34] Cf. Carmelo Musumarra, *Verga minore* (Pisa, 1965), pp. 35-37. Although Musumarra stresses mainly the likeness in theme between the reporters' interests and those of Verga — i.e. "scene carnevalesche," interests in duels and fascinating descriptions of women — we also see a closeness in style. As an example, we would like to quote one of Musumarra's choices and a passage from *Eva*:

> Il corso non fu famoso ed io ebbi da compiangere le povere creature che per recarsi ad un dato convegno, per adempiere un uso consacrato, per non mancare a ciò che forse credesi un obbligo sociale, un sacrificio alla moda o che so io, andarono tutte tremolanti a farsi scarrozzare per lungo tratto della città, a rischio di sciupare la morbidezza della loro epidermide, la lucentezza, e l'ordine delle loro chiome, di tornarsene a casa assiderate, infreddate, ammalate, per la ridicola soddisfazione di gettare ad altri o di vedersi gettare qualche mazzetto di fiori, qualche confetto, o per scambiare qualche convenzionale saluto!
>
> from *Gazzeta d'Italia,* 1867.

Non l'avevo vista più sul palcoscenico, e quando la rividi mi parve tutt'altra! Io comprendo come si possano fare pazzie ... per coteste donne che hanno un pubblico per amante, che ci sbattono sul viso tutte le seduzioni,...e che ci abbruciano gli occhi col lampo della loro bellezza, costringendoci ad affissarle avidamente. — Cotesta voluttà che s'inebbria di suoni, che abbaglia di luce, che sollecita con acri profumi, che vi fa ondeggiare dei veli dinanzi

order to adopt the traditional literary language most consistent with the Florentine society which formed the focus of his literary activity at that time, and whose accent was like a "carezza della parola," — as he states in *Eros* — was willing to subordinate his native dialect.

But, even though Verga had hoped that his stay in Florence would be helpful in rectifying his linguistic and technical skills, outside of some superficial improvements he had little success in fulfilling his ambitions. Although he was correct in stating that style cannot exist outside of the "idea," he failed to recognize that there must be a certain spiritual element, a quintessence, to bind the two. If these works do demonstrate the author's "calore dell'animo" and "tumulto dell'immaginazione" as well as "spontaneità dell'ispirazione," [35] what he still lacks is the "sincerità" [36] of true inspiration. His still insecure preparation did not allow him to dominate from the inside the stylistic material he had at his disposal. He had failed to see that, regardless of the much desired closeness between the spoken and the written language, there is between the two "una profonda diversità di stile" that in the written language always moves toward the "dominio dello spirito sull'istinto della materia." [37] In spite of Russo's statement, it does seem that, at this point, Verga looked at the linguistic problem mainly as a "questione di tecnica lessicale," [38] and this is particularly evident in the first works of this phase, where he seems to be attracted,

---

> alla curiosità spasmodica, che ha il sorriso sfacciato , . . . che idealizza tutte le vostre più sensuali passioni, è mostruosa . . . .
>
> from *Eva*, p. 271.

Note for example, the length of the sentences, the same orating tone with the repetition of the same words, — *per, che, cotesto,* — and the likeness in choice of resounding nouns and adjectives — *tremolanti, morbidezza, epidermide, lucentezza, voluttà, spasmodica.*

[35] Benedetto Croce, *La letteratura della nuova Italia* (Bari, 1922), III, 9.

[36] Terracini, pp. 51, 153. Note his excellent observations on what he considers stylistic "sincerità" to be.

[37] *Ibid.*, p. 57.

[38] L. Russo, *Giovanni Verga*, p. 37. This critic states that for Verga "il problema della lingua fu sempre, non una quistione di tecnica lessicale, ma soltanto un problema di sentimento e di esperienza spirituale, e Firenze fu per lui soltanto *un'altra atmosfera,* l'orizzonte più largo . . . di cui bisognasse *respirare l'aria.*" Having in mind Verga's entire literary parabola, we tend to be in agreement with Russo but when Verga first went to Florence he was, as his novels indicate, also concerned with the lexical problem.

perhaps because of their sound and their conspicuousness, by certain forms and terms that, through their repetitious use and emphasis tend, at times, to lose much of their relevance. Words such as *ebbrezza, delirante, inebbriante, lugubre, febbrile,* are used frequently and in *Una peccatrice,* for example, within the course of three consecutive pages, much stress is placed on the elative form — *devotissimo, fortunatissimo, desolatissimo, scontentissima, carissimo, piacevolissimi, bellissimi.* Until he started to realize that language was a problem of deep feelings and spiritual experiences that in his case he could find only in the language that was traditionally his, he would continue to be a "modest and conventional" writer.

A brief preface to the study about to be undertaken should indicate the basic streams among which Verga incessantly and somewhat freely moves in the handling of his expressive selections: the Sicilian norm, which was the innate part of his linguistic heritage, the Florentine standardized norm to which, as already seen, he was trying to adhere and a more general literary norm that he had assimilated through his formal studies and readings. It should also be readily stated that although Verga was not short of speculative interests, as Santangelo points out, he never did possess the *forma mentis* of the theorist. [39] As far as the linguistic problem was concerned, he had not been consciously aware of the fact that the Sicilian dialect, along with other dialects, had been for some time aligning itself with the Florentine. Even though this process of consolidation had not weakened substantially the fundamental diversity and "tipologia funzionale" [40] of the dialect, it would be fair to assume that these two linguistic trends, to his unawareness, had slowly and somewhat naturally come to co-exist in the author's psyche. It would be futile therefore to attempt to find a "clash" between these two norms. One does not set itself against the other. What exists and what will have to be examined is, to use Chiappelli's term, the "interpenetrazione" [41] of the one into the other.

---

[39] G. Santangelo, *Storia della critica verghiana,* 2nd ed. (1962; rpt. Firenze, 1967), p. 14.
[40] De Mauro, p. 24.
[41] F. Chiappelli, *Nuovi studi sul linguaggio del Machiavelli* (Firenze, 1969), p. 8.

When Verga came to grips with this situation and finally realized that the two linguistic trends were not necessarily antagonistic to each other, his narrative, by means of a more masterful use of the various stylistic elements that he had gradually acquired, became more spontaneous and bold. This is clearly indicated by his later works.

In situating these works in the various currents of the Italian literary scene there are clear indications, as many scholars have noted, [42] that they come closest to the so-called "momento manzoniano." Without wishing to indicate a direct derivation — for this would not be correct — it can be said that Verga leans on the Manzonian tradition not so much from personal inclination as from aesthetic affinity. Indeed Verga kept, artistically, mainly to himself and followed no one's footsteps. The similarities that exist between him and Manzoni [43] can also be found, and often to a greater extent, between Manzoni and many other writers of the time — Nievo, Guerrazzi, D'Azeglio and others. This indicates primarily that the "scuola manzoniana," with its ideas and themes aimed at the present and at the future, had become in Italy a dominant and influential literary institution from which no young and ambitious writer could have disassociated himself completely. Verga was no exception but it should also be remembered that at that time he

---

[42] Lina Perroni's "Inchiesta sull'opere di Giovanni Verga," in *Studi verghiani* (Palermo, 1929), pp. 48-71, shows that most of the critics and scholars polled were of this opinion.

[43] Going into details would mean going outside of the central scope of this chapter. A couple of examples ought to suffice. On the linguistic stratum, Verga too favors the use of what Devoto calls "piani stilistici del racconto," (*Nuovi studi di stilistica,* Milano, 1962, pp. 59-61), something that had been mastered by Manzoni. Verga attempts, and with a degree of success, to keep an accurate distinction between the spheres of the first, second and third person and he — the author-narrator — in the voice of the first person, intervenes only to make mention of his responsibilities and of the documents and facts intrinsic to the development of the story, being always careful however, as Manzoni was, not to interfere with the story's events and characters. In fact, his words "dal canto mio non ho fatto che coordinare i fatti... aggiungendovi del mio soltanto la tinta uniforme che può chiamarsi la vernice del romanzo" (Introduction to *Una peccatrice*) seem to echo Manzoni's "rifare la dicitura." As for subjects, it might also be said, as some believed, that Verga's *Capinera* is a direct descendent of Manzoni's creation of "la monaca di Monza."

was still at the embryonic stage of his career. More significant than the similarities between these two writers are their differences, the basic one being that Verga, still uncertain and tangled in the various modes of expression, moves about, as Luperini has noted, in a D'Annunzio-like style, by way of "accumulazioni, per aggiunte a giustapposizioni,"[44] thus being still quite far from Manzoni's very compact style. In short, what distinguished Verga from Manzoni was artistic maturity. While the latter's immersion in the live language was not only a question of Florentine pronunciation and lexicon, but one of concrete images, "di bernoccoli e lische,"[45] the former's interests still remained at a more superficial level.

In his pursuit of a source of genuine inspiration in harmony with the different norms which he had absorbed and internalized, Verga, in a very meaningful sense, had to experience, on his own personal, linguistic level, what the nation was experiencing on a literary-historical one. Luperini, in fact, does call Verga "scrittore di transizione."[46] He had not yet grasped the historical essence inherent in language. He had to realize that language, in its constant evolutionary process, did not and could not simply ignore the old tradition for the adoption of the new. Rather than through a process of replacement, language has historically functioned through one of addition. This was especially true in Italy where, as already seen, because of its unique social structure, the dialects did not easily give way to a national language. As far as language was concerned, Verga had to come to grips with its historical reality, and, in so doing, he had to pass through a period whose origin was congruent with the "realismo linguistico" of the Manzonian school. Thus, as Ascoli had already acutely noted and urged, Verga was able to arrive at a deeper understanding, evaluation and appreciation of his native norm.

---

[44] Luperini, p. 36.
[45] Devoto, *Profilo,* p. 126.
[46] *Pessimismo e verismo,* pp. 3-4. Luperini calls Verga "scrittore di transizione ... perchè vissuto in un'età di transizione, contrassegnata dal passaggio dallo idealismo romantico dell'Italia risorgimentale al per lo più scettico positivismo dell'Italia borghese, avviata ad un chiaro sviluppo capitalistico, di dopo il '60." We believe that this transitory stage is also evidenced by Verga's language.

PHONOLOGY

1.0.1. In the field of phonology, it can be safely stated that, in general, Verga conforms to the nationally accepted norm, which means adopting primarily the correct pronunciation and orthography as set by the Florentine norm. [1] As to the standard of reference with regard to Florentine usage we have availed ourselves of two sources — Rigutini-Fanfani's *Vocabolario italiano della lingua parlata* (Firenze, 1893) and Fanfani's more generous, as far as number of entries goes, *Vocabolario della pronunzia toscana* (Firenze, 1879) [2] — that verify the orthographic and the orthoepical structure of the forms considered in this study.

There are, however, some variants and certain forms, mostly within the set norm, that place in a clearer focus the author's preferences. This chapter aims at probing and interpreting these preferences through a study of these variants and forms.

1.1.1. Verga makes practically no use of the semi-consonant (or semivowel) *j*, either as an alternate for *i* in an initial or intervocalic position or as a substitute for the-*ii* plural endings (see sec. 2.2.1). This was not the case, however, with *I carbonari della montagna,* [3] where this letter appears with a degree of consistency (e.g., *bajo, annojarsi, gajo, bujo, gioja, acciajo, majuscolo, jeri, ajuto, muojono, cuojo, rejetto, jattanza, bajonetta, Gennajo, ingojava,* etc.). With the fourth and final part of this novel the *j* begins

---

[1] See Malagoli, *Ortoepia e ortografia italiana moderna,* 2nd ed. (Milano, 1912), p. 1.

[2] Herein after we shall refer to these works by their compilers' names: Rigutini-Fanfani for the first and Fanfani for the second.

[3] Written and published in Catania, 4 vols., 1861-62.

to disappear (*bujo* and *gioja,* e.g., have now become *buio* and *gioia*) and the author is quite careful with its use thereafter. One exception, however, is noticed in *Una peccatrice* where, because of a possible oversight, next to the more normal and regarded correct [4] *iena* ("l'urlo della *iena* che ha sentito pungersi"- 56-7), *jena* is also noted ("quella *jena* assetata di vendetta"- 62). *J* also appears in the words *bajadera* (68), *saja* (140, 163, 186) and *rajà* (E.90) but in these cases, its use may be justified by the fact that these words are foreignisms not yet fully absorbed, phonetically, by the Italian system. [5]

Little can be said of the anglicism *jockey* (70, 102, E.143) — a neologism that had been recently adopted [6] — which the author, aware of its foreign origin, presents always in italics.

1.1.1a. By not using this grapheme, it becomes quite clear that Verga, unlike some of his contemporaries and co-regional writers, [7] keeps abreast of the times [8] and, if we are to accept Malagoli's view that in Tuscany the *j* sound does not exist, [9] its absence could also be viewed as an attempt by the author to come closer to the Tuscan norm.

1.2.1. Among the so-called "dittonghi mobili," a considerable amount of oscillation takes place between the diphthong -*ie* and the single -*e*. Although the latter and more modern form prevails, Verga never abandons the more archaic diphthongized structure. This also shows that, for this case at least, the Sicilian influence will always remain with him. [10]

---

[4] See Malagoli, p. 27 (Note): "*Iena* non si scrive con *j*, perchè (proviene) dal latino *hyaena.*"

[5] Even in the Fanfani vocabulary these forms are registered with *j*.

[6] See Rigutini-Cappuccini, *I neologismi buoni e cattivi,* 2nd ed. (Firenze, 1926). See also Migliorini, *Storia,* p. 664.

[7] In this last case we are thinking primarily of Luigi Pirandello, who makes ample use of *j* in his works.

[8] Migliorini, *Storia,* pp. 622-23, states that while the use of *j* is oscillatory in the first half of the 19th Century, a strong regression to its use is evident in the second half of the century.

[9] *Ortoepia,* p. 27.

[10] See A. Traina, *Vocabolarietto delle voci siciliane,* New ed. (Palermo, 1888), p. 12: "Sogliamo in dialetto preporre un *i* all'*e.*"

1.2.2a. With the *altiero-altero* variants, for example, we find that the *-ie* form will yield to the *-e* form. Thus, while *altiero* is most prevalent in the first pages of this production (57, 63, 66, 293), *altero* becomes, later, a very conspicuous replacement (343, 375, 392, E.39, E.47, E.74, E.80, E.86, E.113, et al.). As noun, however, only *alterezza* (403, E.166) is used.

1.2.2b. The distinction of use noticed in the previous case is not present with the variants *intiero-intero*. Although in the later phase it yields considerably to its more conventional counterpart, the archaic *intiero* [11] is noticed throughout this period (52, 64, 86, 92, 95, 128, 170, 279, E.115, et al.). As for examples with *intero* see pp. 264, 336, E.51, E.156, et al. Also present are both *intieramente* (79, 279, E.174) and *interamente* (350, E.183).

1.2.2c. No definite pattern is noticed in the case of *leggiero* and *leggero*. Both forms are used throughout but the former with more frequency: "una *leggiera* tinta d'amarezza" (24), "un *leggiero* movimento" (41), "una *leggiera* convulsione" (67), "corpo *leggiero* da silfide" (68), "donna *leggiera* e capricciosa" (69), "passo *leggiero*" (272), "un *leggiero* scialletto" (283), "un *leggiero* velo" (322), "un tremito *leggiero*" (393), "un *leggiero* strato" (E.10), "mussolina fresca e *leggiera*" (E.43), "una *leggiera* mantellina" (E.170), et al.; also "camminando *leggero leggero*" (45, 182), "mi sentivo più calma, più *leggera*" (172), "il tessuto *leggero*" (E.127). The adverbial form, however, always appears in the monophthongized formation: "Ella era *leggermente* inclinata" (288), "*leggermente* trasparenti" (333), "la voce *leggermente* velata" (353), "inchinò *leggermente* il capo" (E.131).

1.2.2d. The following are further examples with the *-ie* diphthong: *conoscienza* ("in buona *conoscienza* io credo di fare il mio dovere" -377), *coscienza* (137, 207), *passeggiera* ("quelle *passeggiere* preoccupazioni" -372, "le sue passioni [...] erano state così *passeggiere*" - E.81, "una *passeggiera* indisposizione" -E.173). *Superbietta* (E.88, E.163), however, appears along with *superbetta* (E.89); on

---

[11] *Intiero* is registered neither by Rigutini-Fanfani nor by Fanfani.

one occasion *possederò* (30) is preferred to *possiederò* and in one other instance the editor inserts *i* in *picch(i)ettare* (124).

1.2.3. The author is more rigid and conservative in dealing with the *-uo* diphthong. He sticks very closely to the literary norm [12] (*nuovo* and *buono,* i.e., and never *novo* and *bono*), even with the more flexible cases where the diphthong is preceded by the palatal sound. [13] Thus one finds only *spagnuolo* (305), *figliuolo* (45, 361, E.37, et al.), *figliuola* (401, E.15, E.87, E.89, E.141, et al.), *figliuoletto* (138, 166), *famigliuola* (136, 149, 175, 197), *aiuola* (E.33) and *campagnuolo* (E.85).

1.2.3a. *Giuocare* and its various morphological forms are treated, however, with less rigidity. Next to *giuocare* (174, 371), *giuocato* (176), *giuocò* (E.120) and *giuocava* (E.139) found are also *giocare* (E.14, E.89), *giocò* (341), and *giocava* (E.15, E.19, E.24). The substantives *gioco* (E.96) and *giochetti* (77) are less frequent than *giuoco* (286, 291, E.115, E.118) and *giuochi* (279) and the highly unusual *giuocatore* [14] (E.96, E.97) seems to be slightly favored over the more common *giocatore* (E.61). *O* is clearly favored over *-uo* in the case of *giocherellare* (166) and its various forms (*giocherellato* -174, 269, *giocherellando* -E.18); *giuocherellando* appears only once (E.118).

1.2.3b. Very few are the cases with the anomalous monophthongal formations: "il mio *focoso* cavallo" (92), "che hanno un senso comune e che *commovono* tanto" (210), "quell'uomo il quale non si *commoveva*" (E.146), "si *moveva* con contorcimenti" (360).

1.3.1. A degree of conservatism is sensed in the case of the prosthetic forms. Although the prosthetic *i,* for example, was rapidly becoming outdated in the written language — even though it was still popular in the spoken norm of Tuscany especially, [15] — Verga keeps on using some of these forms. In addition to the very con-

---

[12] See Migliorini, *Storia,* p. 625; also Malagoli, p. 35.
[13] See Migliorini, *Storia,* p. 702.
[14] This word appears in neither the Rigutini-Fanfani nor the Fanfani dictionary.
[15] See Migliorini, *Storia,* pp. 626-702; also Malagoli, pp. 156-57.

spicuous *istesso* (see sect. 2.4.16 and 2.4.16a, b), also present are *istanza*[16] (25), *isforzo* (67, 101, 125, E.125), *istrada* (86, 241), *isvegliare* (102), *istupidita* (126, 197), and *istrepito* (145), *iscena* (243), *ischerzo* (335, E.60, E.109), *ispirito* (358), *ismarrire* (E.61), *iscrivere* (E.102).

1.4.1. A few rather uncommon examples of apheresis are also present. In its only appearance, *limosina* (229), a form that was rapidly becoming outdated [17] although it was still popular in the spoken norm, [18] is chosen over the more desirable *elemosine*. The archaic *estraordinario* (*a*) (44, 49, 207) is also present along with the more recurrent *straordinario* (*a*) (42, 57, 301-2, E.89) and *straordinariamente* (55, 301). Most notable is the case of the apheretic *dunque* (30, 51, 53, 138, 151, 273, 370, E.24, et al.), which shares its duty with the more archaic *adunque* (81, 85, 97, 138, 151, 168, E.10, E.103, E.137, et al.).

1.5.1. While the uncommon syncopated forms are very rare (*oprare*-113, is used once in place of *operare*: "Uscii barcollando, operando uno sforzo supremo" -110), more apparent are some of the epenthetic structures. The archaic [19] and already unused *fantasime* (184) makes a single presence while *fantasma* (*i*) (87, 115, 184, 186, 228, 337-8, 394, 408, et al.) predominates by far. *Dirizzare* (67) is, on the other hand, chosen over *drizzare*, *attirare* (329) over *attrarre* and *spasimo* (90, 117, 124, 206, 212, 313) never gives way to the more strictly medical term [20] *spasmo*. In the case of the *fisionomia-fisonomia* variants, Verga, by using only the latter form, clearly follows the prevalent and more popular norm (32, 44, 58, 125, 127, 173, 214, 350, 365, 398, E.154, E.159, E.161, E.178, et al.). [21]

---

[16] *Istanza* is not even preceded by a word ending with a consonant: "unì le sue *istanze* a quelle di Raimondo."

[17] Malagoli, p. 162; also Migliorini, *Storia,* p. 725.

[18] See Rigutini-Fanfani; also Malagoli, p. 162.

[19] See C. Grandgent, *From Latin to Italian* (Cambridge, 1927), p. 67.

[20] See F. Palazzi, *Novissimo dizionario della lingua italiana,* 2nd ed. (Milano, 1964).

[21] See Malagoli, p. 149, and Migliorini, *Storia,* p. 646. In Rigutini-Cappuccini, *Neologismi,* only *fisonomia* is registered.

1.6.1. Several vowel variations are also present. Among the forms where the change occurs on the stressed vowel, *annichilire* (*annichilisce* -188, *annichilito* -195, 301) is less recurrent than the more archaic and literary *annichilare*[22] (*annichilato* -50, 52, 106, 110, 111, *annichila* - E.78, *annichilamento* - 116). The more approved *dimagrata* (327-8, 404) appears with more frequency than *dimagrita*.[23]

1.6.2. The greatest amount of vowel alternation takes place with the vowels in a pretonic position: *A-e* - *Malinconico* (*a*) (86, 111, 170, 191, 236, 409) and *malinconia* (370) are not as current, in these pages, as the older and less used *melancolico*[24] (175, E.47, E.133, E.134, E.160, E.162) and *melanconia* (356). *Garentire* (114) is prefered to *garantire*, *oltraggiare* (E.89) to *oltreggiare*. *Meraviglia* (E.36) appears along with the assimilated and more seldom used *muraviglia*[25] (22). The more conservative form *tristamente* (43, 44, 45, 67, 74, 108, 116, 131, 132, 243, 396, E.135, E.141, E.184, et al.) never gives way to *tristemente*, although *triste* (135, 179, 375, 376, 406 et al.) is — except for the single appearance of *tristo* (175) — the only adjectival form used.

1.6.3. *O-u.* Although *ufficialmente* was rapidly becoming more popular in use than *officialmente*,[26] Verga remains faithful to the more antiquated form (see E.81). As a noun, however, one notices only *ufficiale* (69, 70, 71). A conservative position is taken with the following choices: *Coltura* (20), *soggezione* (357, 363, 370, 402, E.137), *molinello* (363), *formola* (84).[27]

---

[22] Migliorini, *Storia*, p. 167, points out that this form was in use since the 13th Century. Palazzi maintains that this is the more correct form. Malagoli, p. 141, states that the *-are* forms are more literary while the *-ire* ending forms are more conventional.

[23] *Dimagrita* (and *dimagrire*) is not accepted by Malagoli (p. 141) and is not registered by Rigutini-Fanfani. But it does appear in the Fanfani dictionary.

[24] See Malagoli, p. 141.

[25] *Ibid.*, p. 138. This form was still popular in spoken Florentine (see Migliorini, *Storia*, p. 646), but since Verga uses this form only at the beginning of this production we doubt that he may have been influenced by the Florentine spoken norm.

[26] See Migliorini, *Storia*, p. 698.

[27] See Malagoli, p. 146. The tendency was clearly the opposite; *u* was increasingly favored over *o*.

1.6.4. I-e. Some oscillation is present with some forms belonging to this group. *Delicato* (395, 397, E.13, E.17, E.142) prevails although *dilicato* (321) is also present. [28] *Delicatezza* (155, 371, 392, 393, et al.), though, is the only substantival form used. The form *cilestre* [29] (166), perhaps influenced by the Sicilian usage, does make its appearance next to the more conventional *celeste* (207, 208, 398, et al.). Present are also the following double forms: *gittare* (*gittò* -E.47, E.171) and the more conventional *gettare* (226, 229, 301, E.18, E.19, E.171); *assidersi* (175, 301, 352, 411) as well as *assedersi* (180, E.58, E.148, E.152). No phonetic variants are present in the case of *riputazione* (292, 349, E.115, E.116, E.122, E.176, et al.), a form belonging to the popular norm, [30] and *quistione* (236, 237, 291, 363, E.137, et al.), constantly preferred to the learned and more used *questione*. [31] The more archaic form with *e* is favored over the one with *i* in the single appearance of *laberinto* (E.38) and *repugnare* (366, 394-5).

1.6.5. I-a. Insieme (25, 187) is as evident as the Florentine vernacular *assieme* [32] (95, 97, E.43), while the southern oriented *attorno* (66, 111) will later give way to *intorno* (E.48, E.116).

1.6.6. E-u. Except for the appearance of the by now anomalous *equalmente* (E.89) and for the oscillation between *riuscire* (394, E.14) and the different forms of the analogical *riescire* (E.14, E.45, E.97, E.136, E.167), present primarily in the last novel, the author follows quite closely the set norm.

1.6.7. I-o. Although the literary *domandare* (185, 232, 295, 314, 363, E.161) prevails also present is the Florentine phonetic variant *dimandare* [33] (E.141, E.175). *Dimestichezza* (256, E.159) is also present in place of the more conventional *domestichezza*.

---

[28] Cf. Grandgent, p. 37.

[29] This form will be dear to Pirandello.

[30] See Malagoli, p. 144.

[31] See Malagoli, p. 145; also Grandgent, p. 41.

[32] See G. Rohlfs, *Grammatica storica della lingua italiana e dei suoi dialetti: sintassi e formazione delle parole,* trans. T. Franceschi and M. Caciagli Fancelli (Torino, 1969), p. 261.

[33] See Migliorini, *Storia,* p. 612. It might also be possible that this form is carried over from the Sicilian norm. Mortillaro, in his introduction to

1.6.8. Misc. Among the post-tonic forms, both *demonio* and *demone* are present, but the former and more popular form is slightly more frequent: "mi dibatto contro il *Demonio*" (203), "vorrei essere *demonio*!" (207), "questo *demonio* tentatore che si chiama pensiero" (210); "È il *demone* che mi assale" (186), "sente la mano del *demone*" (204), "il *demone* dell'orgoglio" (E.64). The major number of variants is noticed with the various morphological structures deriving from *giovane*: *giovanotto* (81, 155, 303, 370, E.140, et al.), *giovanetto* (*a*) (20, 45, 69, 87, E.20, E.34, E.83), *giovinotto* (211, 368), *giovinetto* (*a*) (314, E.13, E.40, E.67),[34] *giovane* (67, et al.), *giovine* (205), *giovinezza* (285, 299, 397, E.142, et al.).

1.7.1. The Sicilian influence, seen as a conservative power, is very much in evidence in the gemination of certain consonants, especially when these are preceded by *a*.[35] The consonant most often reinforced is *b*.[36] *Abbadare* (381, E.82) strongly overshadows *badare* and *abbadessa* (188, 189, 200, 219, 222), *abbiettezza* (59), *abbiezione* (283) and *abbisognare* (158, 189) clearly dominate over the more conventional *badessa, abiettezza, abiezione* and *bisognare*. Other forms always appearing with *-bb* are: *Inebbriare* (90, 91, 93, 118, 122, 149, 298, et al.),[37] *inebbriante* (44, 47, 84, 85, 90, 116, 121, 251, 263, 264, 294, 296, et al.), *ebbro* (27, 245, 262, 299 et al.),[38] *ebbrietà* (118), *ubbriaco* (230, 231, et al.) and *ubbriacare* (301). *Briaco*, inspired by the spoken Florentine is also evident on a couple of instances (59, 61). Some oscillation takes place with *abbietta* (59, 245) and *abietta* (207) and with *bruciare* (148, 236, et al.) and *abbruciare* (207).

---

his *Nuovo dizionario Siciliano-Italiano*, 3rd ed. (Palermo, 1876), uses this form (p. 3) and he registers *addimannari* (as well as *addomandari*) as Sicilian forms.

[34] These are the prevalent forms in *I carbonari della montagna*.

[35] See Traina, *Vocabolarietto*, p. 11: "È nostro vezzo ... il preporre *a* a molti verbi." We should also point out that Verga also favors *a* before and attached to the conjunction *dunque: adunque*.

[36] *Ibid.*, p. 17: "Alcune consonanti le rinforziamo sempre, come *b, q*." See also in Traina, *Vocabolarietto*, p. 13 and Malagoli, p. 97. These are also considered the more archaic forms: Grandgent, p. 42.

[37] Malagoli, p. 136, states that this form is less popular than *inebriare* and Palazzi considers the single *b* form as the only correct one.

[38] Today, according to Palazzi, this is the only correct form. Fanfani, however, also registers *ebro*.

1.7.2. The form with the double *r* preceded by *a* is often elected to or coexists with its alternate form. *Arrecare* (*arrecava*- 30, 289, *arrecavano*- 263, *arrecavo*- 262, *arreco*- 139) is just as apparent as the conventional *recare* (32, 170) (*recato*- 26, *recando*- E.140); *arrovesciare* (382, 384, E.108, E.115) is decisively preferred to *rovesciare* (300), and *arrischiare* (160, 287, 303, E.174) completely obliterates *rischiare*. It may be due to the inclination toward the use of the double consonant that *arrivederci* (253, E.169), a form that had not yet become common, [39] appears along with the more widely used *a rivederci* (38, 354, 365, 378, 403).

1.7.3. Oscillation also exists with the *-cc* verbal forms. *Carezzare* (22, 25, 90, E.85) is as notable as the more common *accarezzare* (139, 182, 297, E.41, E.56 et al.) while the popular *accontentare* yields completely to *contentare* (294, 403).

1.7.4. Here are further examples of *a+ double consonants* that may be attributed to the Sicilian tradition. *Addomesticare* ("colla grazia di una gazzella *addomesticata*"- E.54) is, for example, preferred to *domesticare*; *assedersi* and *assidersi* (see sec. 1.6.4.) are present along with the much more customary *sedersi*. *Attraversare* (200, 269, 355, E.143) and *traversare* (115, 156, 397) are both present, and so are *noiato* (356, 399) and *annoiarsi* (E.21, E.140). The *fisare-fissare-affissare* group deserves a closer look. The various forms — transitive and reflexive — of these three verbs are of notable prevalence and are often used interchangeably to imply an identical meaning. This is certainly true of *fissare* especially, the most widely used of all three forms, and *affissare*. The fluctuation in use between these two verbs is quite common, as Leone clearly implies, [40] in the Sicilian norm. Here are some examples: "Mi *affissò* un istante" (231), "gli occhi della madre che ti *affissano* in volto" (234), "mi *affissò* con certi occhi" (260), "uno sguardo (...) si *fissò* (...) negli occhi ardenti di Pietro" (27), "Ella *fissò* un lungo sguardo su quello che si fissava su di lei" (68), "onde *fissarsi* ancora su di Pietro" (124), "a *fissare* gli occhi nel firmamemto"

---

[39] *Arrivederci* is registered neither by Fanfani nor by Rigutini-Fanfani.
[40] "Di alcune caratteristiche dell'Italiano di Sicilia," *Lingua Nostra*, XX (1959), 90. (Henceforth *Lingua Nostra* shall appear in the abbreviated form *L. N.*).

(151), "il suo sguardo *fissò* su di me" (155), "*fissò* su di Giorgio (...)
uno sguardo limpido" (325). For further examples with *fissare* see
pp. 32, 40, 48, 235, 350, et al.; for *fisare* see pp. 383, 387, 397,
408, 409, E.9, E.11, E.80, et al. and for *affissare* see pp. 248, 262.

1.7.5. To make, at this point, a marginal stylistic observation,
it should be stated that Verga is particularly fond of the *a+ double
consonant* forms in describing love scenes both in *Tigre reale* and
Eros. These forms acquire a phonostylistic value for they are used
to strengthen the emotive meaning of the entire scenes. They help,
in other words, in suggesting a strong, if not violent, clinging desire
that invades the mind of the "femmes fatales" involved. In the case
of Nata, for example, in her last moments prior to her death, she
wants to be the sole and avid possessor of Giorgio and this attitude
is accentuated through the selected use of verbs such as *avventarsi*
("gli si *avventò* al collo con un che di selvaggio" -382), *abbando-
narsi* ("gli si *abbandonò* nelle braccia" -382), *arrovesciare* ("col capo
arrovesciato all'indietro" -382), *avviticchiare* ("gli si *avviticchiava* al
collo" -383), *appoggiare* ("gli *appoggiava* la testa in seno" -383),
attirare ("Nata all'improvviso *attirò* bruscamente il capo di lui"
-383), and *annaspare* ("*annaspando* colle mani verso il letto" -384).
The definite function of these verbs is further illustrated by Nata's
statement "Hai preso moglie?" Verga is careful in this case not
to use, as he has done on other occasions, the verb *ammogliarsi*,
for it would be in conflict with the intended meaning of seizure
— solely on Nata's part — that these verbs carry.

In *Eros,* in the love scene between Alberto and countess Armandi, one finds that countess Armandi, not unlike Nata, "*arrovesciò* il capo all'indietro (...) e all'improvviso gli si *avventò* al
collo, e lo baciò rabbiosamente." (115).

1.7.6. While there is a decisive preference of *-mm* in the com-
bined *giammai* (9, 10, 40, 45, 60, 92, 95, 101, 117, 219, 228, 279,
289, 295, 312, 314, 358, 359, 395, E.68, E.71, E.100, E.116, et al.)
and in *ammodo* (303, 325, E.28, E.81, E.92, E.133), oscillatory are
the *m-mm* variants in the various structures based on *immagine*.
Although the *-mm* forms prevail in these pages as well as in the
general norm, [41] the *-m* forms are not forgotten here. Thus *imagi-*

---

[41] See Malagoli, pp. 127, 133.

nazione (46), as well as *immaginazione* (21, 290, 327, 397, et al.);
imaginare (135, 137) as well as *immaginare* (160, 196, 213, 394, et
al.); *imagine* (227) as well as *immagine* (129, 334, 397, 399, 409,
et al.).

1.7.7. A degree of oscillation takes place with the use of the
single and double consonants in structures with prepositions as
prefixes. In the case of *da* followed by the explosive *p*, Verga,
unlike the Sicilian tradition,[42] does not always reinforce the consonant. While *dappoi* (59) and *dappresso* (22) are never replaced
by *da poi* and *da presso, da principio* (252) and *da prima* (E.77),
on the contrary, can be seen next to the more frequent *dapprinci-
pio* (59, 141) and *dapprima* (354, E.26, E.103, E.148, E.149). The
same is also true of *da per tutto* (301, E.164) and the much more
favorite *dappertutto* (20, 69, 146, 358, E.71, E.110, E.141, E.142,
et al.).

The fact that *da capo* (161, 408) never appears in its reinforced
form may be due to the Sicilian aversion to the gemination of
certain consonants, as Leone has noticed,[43] that the national language expects to have reinforced.

1.7.8. With *di* as prefix, a great deal of vacillation takes place
between *di già, digià* and the much more conspicuous *diggià* (for
examples and pages see sec. 2.7.3). The Sicilian influence is most
evident in the case of *dippiù*,[44] never replaced by *di più* and very
much present throughout this period (see, e.g., pp. 16, 23, 69, 71,
96, 151, 189, 339, 349, 355, 384, E.41, E.116, E.170, E.179, et al.).
There is, however, some oscillation between the Sicilian affected
eppoi (150),[45] and *e poi* (370). *Appena*, on the other hand, yields
totally to *a pena* (72, 128).

---

[42] See L. 1, Ascoli, "L'Italia dialettale," *Archivio Glottologico Italiano,*
VIII (1882-85), 113.

[43] Leone, "Alcune caratteristiche," p. 30.

[44] Traina, p. 16, makes it a point to state that the Sicilians emphasize *p*
in *più* (thus making it *ppiù*). In addition, we found that neither Rigutini-
Fanfani nor Fanfani register this form.

[45] Traina, p. 17, states that the Sicilian norm, like the standard Italian
norm, favors the doubling of the consonant after *e*.

1.7.9. Both Leone and Traina state that the Sicilian norm does not favor the reinforcement of the consonant when *sopra* is the prefix. [46] The oscillation found in these pages between the single and the double consonant might be seen as the result of the author's inability to break away rapidly from a custom that was part of his native norm. Thus present are *sopranominata* (33), *soprapensiero* (E.46), *sopratutto* (90, 185, 379) as well as *soprannominare* (E.39, E.142) and *soprappensieri* (E.178). The following forms, however, always appear with the double consonant: *sopraffina* (85), *soprammercato* (E.14) and the various verbal forms of *sopraggiungere* ("*sopraggiunse* mia sorella" - 158, "della natura che *sopraggiunge*, com'è *soppraggiunto* l'inverno"- 170), *sopravvenire* (E.58) (*sopravviene*- 188, *sopravvennero*- 328), *sopraccaricare* (*sopraccaricarono*- 174), and *sopraffare* (377) (*sopraffatto*- 346). There are also instances where the second consonant is added by the editor in brackets: *sopra[n]naturale* (69), *sopra[c]ciglia* (121), *sopra[p]pensieri* (372). The editor also intervenes in one instance with *contra* as prefix: *contra[d]dizione* (311).

1.7.10. With the prefix *intra*, the double consonant (*v*) appears only once ("far *intravvedere* alla moglie"- 166) while most times the single consonant is used: *intravide* (53), *intravedere* (74), *intravedevasi* (E.156). The single consonant also follows the prefix *così*: *cosifatta* (E.167).

1.7.11. There are other cases where the double consonant is favored: *profferire* (84) is favored to *proferire*, the literary *retorica* [47] gives way to the popular *rettorica* (225) and also present is the widely used — but, phonetically, erroneously arrived at [48] — *libriccino* (171). The double consonant is sometimes used in verbal forms with alternate structure: *veggo* (136, 154, 178, 179, et al.), *veggono* (86), *chieggo* (199). The single consonant is applied, on the other hand, to *inoltrare* (E.68, E.158).

---

[46] Leone, op. cit., p. 90. Also Traina, *Vocabolarietto*, p. 17: "non rinforziamo le consonanti precedute da ... sopra."

[47] See Malagoli, p. 137.

[48] *Ibid.*, p. 148.

1.8.1. With respect to other kinds of consonant variations, we find that, in the *c-g* group, by adopting only *lagrime* (45, 46, 75, 90, 96, 106, 131, 133, 137, 162, 311, 322, E.157, et al.), Verga displays a conservative [49] and a typically Sicilian [50] position. Oscillatory is the case of *sagrifizio* (86, 105, 115), present only at the beginning of this period and remaining, in the long run, a poor second to *sacrificio* (85, E.135, E.141, E.150, E.159, et al.) and *sacrificare* (*si*) (86, 117, et al.).

1.8.2. It appears that, as a general rule, Verga tends to lean away, wherever possible, from the *-izio* endings: *servigio* (241, 324, 354), therefore, and not *servizio, artificio* (337) (and *artifici-* 399) and not *artifizio.*

1.8.3. To the Sicilian norm might be attributed two examples, early in this period, where *d* is inverted and preferred to *t* in *nudrire*: [51] "la viva amicizia che *nudriva* pel suo compagno" (25), "il culto che *nudriva* della madre" (45). A conservative attitude is also shown with other forms where the less common consonant takes the place of the more generally accepted one. *Cangiare,* for instance, is very evident: "mi trovo così *cangiata*!" (152), "riflessi *cangianti*" (334), "era sempre *cangiante* e bizzarro" (337), "nell' ombra sembravano *cangiare*" (409). The archaic *covrire* ("*covrendolo* quasi col suo largo petto"- 56) also appears and so does *riserbatezza* (E.142). The apheretic *trascinare* (27, 44, 290) remains second to the stronger and perhaps Sicilian influenced *strascinare* [52] (115, 123, 128, 197) and the *-tz* combination in *valtzer* (49, 51, 122, 125, et al.) will eventually give way to *z* (*valzer*: E.45, E.47).

1.9.1. In conclusion, the Battaglia-Pernicone grammar notes that Verga favors marking the accent on words that have the *-io* and *-ia* stressed endings. [53] Although this is generally true, a closer look reveals that Verga is not consistent with this practice. While

---

[49] *Ibid.,* p. 148.

[50] Traina, *Vocabolarietto,* pp. 14 and 15, states that Sicilian norm often prefer *g* to *c*; *lagrima* is one of these cases.

[51] See Leone, p. 90; also Traina, *Vocabolarietto,* p. 14.

[52] See Rigutini-Fanfani.

[53] Torino, 1960, p. 48.

the accent appears on forms such as *ginguettìo* (140, E.25), *ronzìo* (147, 153, E.18), *brulichìo* (193), *bramosìe* (240), *sussurrìo* (240), *frenesìe* (262), *civetterìa* (295), *follìe* (334, E.161), *tintinnìo* (407), *leggìo* (E.50), and *mugolìo* (E.63), no accent is placed on *bizzarria* (325), *leggiadria* (E.17), and *pazzia* (E.32). In other instances the accent is sometimes shown and at other times it is not: *fruscìo* (150, 260, 261, 406, E.46, E.169, et al.) and *fruscio* (89), *mormorìo* (E.182, E.185) and *mormorio* (55, 170), *scalpiccìo* (E.185) and *scalpiccio* (E.184).

MORPHOSYNTAX

2.1.1. Sometimes the definite article appears in an anomalous position. It is found before nouns denoting close relatives and even before the possessives preceding such nouns: "*La* mamma Ruscaglia era sempre per casa" (367), "*la* mamma Manfredini si era mostrata più preoccupata del solito" (E.79), "sono *la tua* sorella" (218), "farai quello che ti dice di fare *la tua* zia" (402). Once the article also appears before a clerical title followed by a proper name: "penso *al* padre Anselmo" (154).

2.1.2. The influence of the spoken Florentine becomes evident with the numerous examples where the article, alone or attached to the preposition, precedes the feminine names: [1] *l'*Adele, *la* Velleda, *la* Gegia, *l'*Agatina, *l'*Emilia, *l'*Irma, *colla* Irma, *colla* Lina, *all'*Adele, and so on. On one occasion the article is also found before a male noun: "amo sempre *il* Nino!" (210). This form appears with increasing frequency and it will last well into the major works (cf. i.e. in *I Malavoglia*: *la* Lia, *la* Santuzza, etc.).

2.1.3. The presence of the article before the names of months, holidays and times of day is also not unusual: "Ieri fu *il* Natale" (174), "per fare *il* Natale colla sua famigliuola" (175), "hanno giocato sino *alla* mezzanotte" (176), "ci sarò fra *il* giugno ed *il* luglio" (330), "verso gli ultimi *del* giugno" (412), "Alberto rientrò

---

[1] See Raffaello Fornaciari, *Sintassi italiana dell'uso moderno,* 2nd ed. (Firenze, 1884), p. 128; also Gerhard Rohlfs, *Sintassi e formazione delle parole,* p. 30. (In this chapter we shall use the above mentioned book of Rohlfs as well as his volume on *Morphology,* Tran. T. Franceschi [Torino, 1968]. Herein after we shall refer to them as *Sintassi* and *Morfologia* respectively).

verso *il* mezzogiorno" (E.65), "il matrimonio era stato fissato *pel* settembre" (E.84).

2.1.4. In the exclamations the article is occasionally a substitute for the more conventional *che.* Russo[2] attributes this vocative trait to the Sicilian norm. Thus, "*La* bella donna!" (15), "*La* brava gente!" (146), "Oh, *il* bel fiorellino!" (E.26), "*La* bella signora!" (E.45), "*il* buon dottore!" (E.183).

2.1.5a. More conspicuous are the instances where the article, either definite or indefinite, is missing. *Un* and *una* are often omitted, especially before *certo* (*a*): "di *certa* Palmira che avea rapito ai trionfi del San Carlo" (320), "i movimenti di lei avevano *certa* elasticità carezzevole" (E.17), "sentiva dentro di sé *certo* mugolìo" (E.63), "avea *certa* voluttà" (E.136) and "per la quale avrebbe dato altra volta tutto il suo sangue" (52), "l'altra notte udii rumore nel suo appartamento" (93), "Tutt'a un tratto si udì rumore" (166), "hai fatto buon Natale?" (176), "mi avea detto altra volta" (270), "confusione di pensiero che sento in così fragile involucro" (312), "con accento che spezzava il cuore" (314), "riprese dopo breve pausa" (E.25), "rispondeva a lui con voce piena di una dolce sonorità" (E.40), "Lo zio tacque maestosamente, aspettando risposta per alcuni secondi" (E.57).

2.1.5b. In fewer instances, *la* is also missing: "i contadini udirono abbaiare tutta notte" (E.65), "Ascoltava messa tutti i giorni" (E.86). Special attention should be given to the unique case, in *Storia di una capinera,* where *la* is missing before *mia matrigna.* The explanation lies within the psychological and stylistic realm. By way of analogy, Maria, the protagonist of the story, regards her stepmother as her own mother and as a consequence of this *matrigna,* when preceded by the possessive, is treated similarly to the word *madre. Mia matrigna* (163, 182, 183, 189, 202 et al.), therefore, by far exceeds *la mia matrigna* (135, 139).

2.1.5c. The article is also found omitted after the relative particle *come* followed by *cera*: "Bianche come cera" (333), "pallida come cera" (344, E.93, E.128, et al.), "candida come cera" (361).

---

[2] *Verga,* p. 285.

2.1.6. On one occasion *uno* is replaced by the rather anomalous form *un*: "mormorò Alberti con *un* strano sorriso" (E.147). More cases of the sort will be evidenced when *uno* acts as a pronoun (see 2.4.17).

· *2.1.7.* Verga takes a rather conservative attitude with the combination of certain prepositions with the definite article. While the contractions *con* and *per* + *article* were rapidly falling into disuse [3] Verga persists in favoring them over the uncombined forms: "*pel* primo" (19), "*cogli* accenti" (20), "*colle* lagrime" (20), "*colle* carezze" (20), "*colla* società" (20), *collo* scintillare" (61), "*pei* vasti corridoi" (190), "*pel* mio ingegno" (240), *colla* catena del matrimonio al collo" (363), "*pel* colore locale" (246), "*cogli* improvvisi rossori" (E.40), "andarono *pel* viale" (E.42), et al.

2.2.1. A degree of conservativism is also shown, at times, with the plural double -*i* ending forms. [4] Although rapidly disappearing they appear in these works in their various orthographic endings: with the double -*i*, circumflex accent or with the more updated single -*i*. Thus one sees *desiderî* (138, 240, 245, 293, 300, 311, 392, 399) next to *desideri* (225, E.48), *delirî* (171) next to *delirii* (66), *serî* (184) as well as *seri* (275, 237, E.81), *dubbî* (103, 374) along with *dubbi* (153, 208, E.151) *demonî* (207) as well as *demoni* (208, 210). Also: *esempî* (20), *studî* (25, E.14), *uffizî* (140), *silenzî* (140), *sucidî* (E.150), *principî* (275, 394), *auqurî* (322), *artificî* (399), *esercizî* (207), *anniversarii* (57), *sacrifizii* (115), *precipizii* (112), *negozii* (E.68), but *effluvi* (293), *annunzi* (287), *corridoi* (141, 190), *straordinari* (E.89), *vizi* (E.86), *gai* (E.142), *usurai* (293).

2.2.2. With the nouns that may take a double ending in the plural, only one form is usually used: *cervella* (118, 258, 380), for example, is always preferred to *cervelli* as *lenzuoli* (196) to *lenzuola*. This is not the case, however, with *ginocchi* which, although used with much less frequency, appears along with *ginocchia*: "coi

---

[3] See Fornaciari, *Grammatica italiana dell'uso moderno*, 2nd ed. (Firenze, 1882), pp. 78-79, and Giuseppe Finzi, *Grammatica italiana* (Torino, 1911), p. 27.

[4] "Se il singolare termina in *io*, allora, per regola generale, si mettono nel plurale due *i*": Fornaciari, *Gramm. ita.*, p. 86.

gomiti sui *ginocchi*" (43), "venne a posare la sua grossa testa sui miei *ginocchi*" (156), "gli teneva il capo sui *ginocchi*" (307); "venne a sedermi sulla *ginocchia*" (268), "finiva saltandomi sulle *ginocchia*" (263), "mi sentii piegar le *ginocchia*" (169), "colle mani incrociate sulle *ginocchia*" (170), "mi tengo sulle *ginocchia*" (177), "le nostre *ginocchia* si toccavano" (258), et al.

2.2.3. In the cases where abstract forms are extended to the concrete and are usually placed in the plural, Verga seems to favor the singular: "di non guardare il precipizio per non avere *la vertigine*" (113), "aggrottò *il sopracciglio*" (E.9, E.87).

2.2.4. As for other alternate forms, somewhat peculiar is the choice of the masculine pejorative *paroloni* over the more common *parolone* ("quei fantasmi che voi altri avete creato a furia di *paroloni!*" -311) and equally interesting are the various alternate forms applied to *giovane*: *giovanotto* (81, 155, 303, E.141), *giovanetto* (45, 86, 87, 69), *giovinotto* (211, 368), *giovinetto* (E.13), *giovinetta* (314, E.40), *giovanetta* (E.20, E.34, E.83), *giovanettino* (342).

2.2.5. Among the names of animals used in the figurative sense, conspicuous is the use of *serpe* in the masculine: "quel *serpe* l'ho sempre qui" (203), "quasi un *serpe* l'avesse morsicato" (311). Once, *Czar* is used in place of the fem. *Czarina*: "amico personale della *Czar*" (331).

2.3.1. If these novels — the first two especially — can be best characterized by a single part of speech, it would have to be the very conspicuous presence of the adjectives. This situation may be seen, at least in part, as the result of the "lingua altamente decorosa" [5] sought in the prose of the first half of the 19th century. Verga's own expressive limitations should not also be overlooked. Thinking, perhaps, of a decorous language as synonymous with desirable and attractive prose, he does not hesitate to fill his narrative with attributives.

As can be anticipated, there are many qualifying adjectives deriving from the present and past participles. The following is

---

[5] B. Migliorini, *Storia,* p. 595.

but a small sample of adjectives of a somewhat outlandish nature: *abbagliante, affascinante, anelante, ardente, delirante, desolante, divorante, febbricitante, fervente, fiammeggiante, fluttuante, inebbriante, irritante, lacerante, languente, palpitante, penetrante, provocante, pungente, rovente, scintillante, seducente, sfavillante, sfolgorante, sfrenante, smaniante, spasimante, straziante, trepidante* and *agitato, allampanato, annichilato, annichilito, assetato, avvinazzato, dimagrata, dissimulata, disperato, esulcerata, fatata, illividita, imbellettata, infuocato, pacato, profumato, stralunato, trafelato.*

2.3.2. Often the role of the adjective is intensified with the help of adverbs of quantity. *Assai* is the form that most times precedes the adjective: "*assai* bruno (27), "*assai* distinta" (39), "*assai* comuni" (41), "*assai* grande" (55), "*assai* applaudito" (70), "*assai* commossa" (103), "*assai* più pura della mia" (138), "*assai* modesta" (282), "*assai* ridicolo" (336), "*assai* diverse" (E.14), "*assai* strano" (E.158). On rarer occasions and only in the direct discourse, *assai* follows the adjective: "malinconica *assai*" (170), "simpatico *assai*" (E.29). In comparison, there are relatively few examples with *troppo* and even fewer with *molto*: "*troppo* superiore" (19), "*troppo* piccolo compenso" (87), "*troppo* brutto e *troppo* serio" (330), "era *troppo* gran dama" (E.94); "*molto* magra" (336), "*molto* giovane" (E.138).

2.3.3. The absolute superlatives are used with much discretion and they acquire meaning primarily on the stylistic level. In *Una peccatrice,* for example, a conglomeration of superlatives is found within three pages. They are all associated with a mood of elation that the speakers experience at that particular instant while referring, in one way or another, to the heroine of the story: *devotissimo, fortunatissimo, desolatissima, scontentissima* (all on p. 80), *carissimo* (81), *piacevolissimo* (82), *bellissimi* (82). In *Storia di una capinera* the many superlatives have to be seen in connection with the main character's altered and childishly innocent psychological state. Numerically, this story contains the largest number of superlatives: *dolcissime* (133), *modestissimo* (140), *indulgentissimi* (149), *intimissimi* (154), *buonissimo* (154), *cortesissimo* (154), *sciocchissimo* (156), *innocentissima* (156), *cattivissima* (159), and so on. In the other novels the superlatives are more rarely used: *pallidissimo* (231), *amarissimo* (236), *dispiacentissima* (326), *debolissima* (334), *riconos-centissima* (334), *piacevolissima* (355), *capricciosissima* (E.79) et al.

2.3.4. The position of the adjective generally follows the conventional norm. Usually the epithetic and attributive adjectives — often appearing in sets of two or three — immediately follow the substantives: "cavalieri *giovani, ricchi, eleganti*" (61), "signore *belle, profumate, splendenti*" (61), quella *brutta, cinica, briaca, cenciosa*" (61), "donna *volubile, galante, appassionata e impetuosa*" (82), "il vero senso *appassionato, addolorato, ansioso*" (106), "donna *calma, serena*" (138), "donniciuola *infermiccia* ed *uggiosa*" (191), "affetto *vergine e schietto*" (E.151) and so on.

2.3.5. In the predicative role the adjective always follows the subject and the verb, although at times there might be a subordinate clause between them: "Egli fu *freddo, distratto, impacciato*" (67), "si è arrestato *anelante, spossante*" (87), "mi pare debba essere *terribile, divorante*" (87), mi baciava *frenetico, ardente*" (98), "ero *sbalordita, astratta, trasognata*" (137), "era *timida, triste, malaticcia*" (131), "rimasi (...) appoggiato al caminetto, *duro, pallido, fosco*" (277).

2.3.6. Nevertheless, the conventional position of the adjectives, like those of the word-order, cannot be strictly observed in all cases; there is a certain freedom of movement, which reflects a similar movement in the mind of the writer or speaker. It appears, therefore, that attributives are sometimes found before, rather than after, nouns when what is being accentuated is the notional vividness of certain objects, appearances, persons and attitudes: "La mia matrigna è un'*eccellente* donna" (135), "*cattivi* e *barbari* divertimenti" (141), "che *magnifico* spettacolo!" (144), "*infantile* vivacità" (250), "Che *piccole* mani avete, signore!" (250), "piena di *acri* fumi e di *inesplicabili* attrattive" (338), "un'*indefinibile* commozione" (400), "domandò Alberto con *ironico* sorriso" (E.150), "*amara* e *tranquilla* convinzione" (E.150), "*umane* passioni" (E.150).

2.3.7. There are other cases where the position of the adjective seems to reflect the mannerisms of the drawing room society that the author is describing. In some phrases denoting time, for example, the adjective almost systematically appears in an order opposite to what the general practice would have it. *Scorso,* for instance, precedes rather than follow the noun: "Uno degli *scorsi* giorni" (155), "Tutta la *scorsa* notte non ho potuto dormire" (191); *parecchie* always follows *ore*: "Alberto stette inutilmente delle ore *parecchie*" (E.27), "li allontanavano inesorabilmente per delle ore *parecchie*" (E.159); and *altro* appears more often after than before the temporal adverb *ieri*: "*L'altro* ieri (...) le domandai il permesso di abbracciarla" (140), but "Frattanto ieri *l'altro* (...) vidi un'ombra alla finestra" (157), "mi ha chiesto di lei ier *l'altro*" (324), "Ier *l'altro* l'ho vista a Firenze" (E.73).

2.3.8a. While most times the possessive adjectives comply with the general usage — by preceding the noun to which they refer —,[6] there are cases where, for accentuating purposes, they follow: "per l'inusitata e straordinaria tardanza del figlio *suo*" (42), "che ritrovava il figlio *suo*" (64), "la felicità del figlio *suo*" (90), "che aveva pur diritto all'amore del figlio *suo*" (104), "Il padre *suo* insisteva per accompagnarmi sino allo stradale" (315), "di domandare del figlio *suo*" (391).

2.3.8b. At times, although rarely, the possessive precedes the noun while the more common order would require the opposite. With *casa,* for example, the possessive usually follows ("per andare a casa *sua*" -36), but one also sees: "Sono stata in *sua* casa due o tre volte" (35), "Brusio era ritornato a *sua* casa agitatissimo" (71). The same holds true with *colpa*: "vedrai che (...) non fu *mia* colpa" (147), "Non è *mia* colpa se è stato più forte di me" (410). In this last case, this particular word-order brings to mind the liturgical "mea culpa" and in the first example quoted this may well be the case since Maria, in *Storia di una capinera,* has lived in a convent and is destined to become a nun.

2.3.9. Verga is always very careful in erasing all ambiguities in instances where the possessive might apply to more than one person. When the case arises the possessive is accorded to the subject and *di* + *personal pronoun* to the object. Often, however,

---

[6] Battaglia-Pernicone, *Grammatica italiana,* 2nd ed. (Torino, 1960), p. 200.

the switch from one form to the other is somewhat unwarranted since the contextual clarity places no doubt on the intended meaning. Here are a few examples:

> Verso le undici entrò Nata, elegante come sempre, ma avea gli occhi profondamente solcati, ed era imbellettata-Giorgio dal suo posto sorprese uno squardo circolare *di lei* sulla folla. (329)

> Nata si voltò come una leonessa ferita; mosse le labbra due o tre volte senza dir nulla e si svincolò vivamente dalle mani *di lui*. (345)

> Verso l'alba l'inferma cominciò ad essere agitata. Giorgio seguiva i movimenti *di lei* con sguardo ansioso, senza osar di fiatare. (409-19)

> L'indomani andò a trovare la moglie e s'informò più minutamente della salute *di lei*. (E.175)

2.3.10. Among the demonstrative adjectives, the archaic *cotesto* (but rarely the more literary *codesto*) is very much favored. There is no doubt that the adoption of this form is the direct result of the Tuscan (and Florentine) influence. Aside from Leone's statement that "l'italiano di Sicilia non usa nè *cotesto* nè *costì*,"[8] one notices that, in spite of its frequent use throughout this period, this form does not appear in *Una peccatrice,* the first of these novels. The reason might very well be that this novel was conceived and perhaps completely written, even if not revised, when the author was still living in his native Catania. It seems, therefore, that with this adjective the author adheres to the spoken Tuscan but also reveals through his use of the archaic form a conservative attitude within the bounds of the Tuscan norm.

The preference for this form is such that often — if not most times — it goes beyond the strict normal sense of indicating the actual or figurative distance of an object, person or thought from the speaker. It becomes, in other words, a replacement for the more conventional *questo* and *quello*. The examples are too many to

---

[7] "La forma *cotesto* è più usata nelle parlate popolari toscane": Rohlfs, *Sintassi,* p. 22.

[8] A. Leone, "Caratteristiche dell'italiano di Sicilia," p. 86.

enumerate and the following is a brief list of pages where examples are found: 134, 135, 136, 137, 151, 152, 153, 155, 162, 171, 175, 177, 182, 233, 234, 235, 236, 237, 238, 244, 255, 257, 262, 263, 270, 271, 280, 291, 294, 311, 312, 321, 323, 325, 347, 382, 402; in *Eros*: 14, 15, 24, 28, 32, 44, 53, 55, 70, 73, 86, 115, 121, 138, 139, 149, 156.

2.4.1. As subject pronouns for the third person singular masculine, in addition to *egli* and *lui,* the form *ei,* always appearing at the beginning of the sentence, becomes increasingly popular and it will also be well in evidence in the mature works. [9] Here it begins to appear with certain consistency in *Tigre reale* and it predominates in *Eros*: "*Ei* le strinse la mano" (371), "*Ei* la baciava" (382), "*Ei* la fissava attentamente" (398), "*Ei* si levò" (410), "*Ei* rispose con accento da Otello" (E.30), "*Ei* rimase (...) pensieroso" (E.36), "*Ei* chinò il capo" (E.46), "*Ei* la trovò su quel sedile" (E.53), "*Ei* s'alzò" (E.112), et al. This form, very popular with the spoken Tuscan but archaic in the literary norm [10] and practically unknown in Southern Italy, [11] indicates, as with the case of *cotesto* (see 2.3.10), a literary conservative attitude within the bounds of the Tuscan norm. Best proof of this is the fact that this form will be dear to the author even after the Florentine period.

2.4.2. *Egli* and the objective *lui* are indiscriminately used as subjects, although *lui* comes to gain a very slight upper hand. Even here, however, the change is so minimal that the author's attitude must be considered as being somewhat conservative, especially when one recalls Manzoni's decision to replace *egli* with *lui* whenever possible. [12]

2.4.3. *Ella* is the most preferred form among the feminine third person pronouns. *Lei,* as subject form, will always remain, regardless of its increase in use, always a poor second: "*Ella* non dev'essere siciliana" (16), "che *ella* udiva sbadatamente" (31), "*Ella* si toglieva (...) a lunghi intervalli" (31), "*Ella* gli sorride" (36), "*Ella*

---

[9] "*Ei* è caro al Verga": Migliorini, *Storia,* p. 705.
[10] See Trabalza-Allodoli, *La grammatica degl'italiani* (Firenze, 1938), p. 131; also Fornaciari, *Sintassi,* p. 237.
[11] See Rohlfs, *Morfologia,* pp. 141-42.
[12] See D'Ovidio, *La lingua dei Promessi sposi* (Napoli, 1933), p. 60.

si alza" (36), "*Ella* gli fissò (...) uno sguardo attonito" (328), "*Ella* si scosse" (371), "*Ella* rispose appena" (E.107), "*Ella* chinò il capo" (E.145), et al.

2.4.4. Also present are the pronouns *essa* and the archaic *dessa,* the latter having a minimal appearance; only in the first and last novels: "È *dessa!*" (31), "No! esclamò *dessa*" (E.65 and E.171). Except, perhaps, for the first example, this pronoun does not necessarily function, as the norm seems to imply, [13] as a reinforcing form of the personal pronoun. Here it serves as an affectedly elegant substitute for a more standard personal pronoun.

Essa appears with much more regularity and is used, most times, as an alternate for another pronoun: [14] "*Essa* non ha la bellezza regolare" (22), "*Essa* cercò tastoni il campanello" (259), "esclamò *essa* con quel riso da bambina" (268), "Erminia non aveva dormito neppur *essa*" (405), "*Essa* tremava un po'" (E.33), "*Essa* ballava in modo singolare" (E.46). Rarely is this pronoun used when referring to a thing instead of a person: "Se gli uomini sapessero far valere questa parola quanto *essa* la merita" (24), "Avevano rivisto insieme quell'anticameretta (...) che non sembrava più quella neppur *essa.*" (371).

2.4.5. *Esso,* on the other hand, is used only to indicate a thing or animal: "Un convoglio funebre (...) *Esso* era semplicissimo" (9), "*Esso* mi saltava addosso latrando" (162), "a quel sogno (...) ch'*esso* era troppo bello" (30).

2.4.6. For the third person plural *essi* is used with much less frequency than *loro*: "*Essi* battevano le mani ai bei colpi" (57), "*Essi* si parlavano da mezz'ora" (E.42).

2.4.7. For the second person singular, both familiar and polite, the entire spectrum, ranging from *tu* to *ella,* is used. These forms are, generally speaking, used according to the general usage. [15] The

---

[13] Cf. Rohlfs, *Morfologia,* pp. 210-11.
[14] Here it does not necessarily carry the original meaning intended by Fornaciari of hinting at "la identità di una cosa o una persona con sè medesima." (*Grammatica,* pp. 128-29).
[15] Cf. Petrocchi, *Grammatica della lingua italiana* (Milano, 1909), pp. 134-35.

author, however, also applies them to denote the various moods and dispositions of the characters. *Tu*, for example, aside from cases implying close intimacy and affection (e.g., in *Eva*, 260-261) or old and renewed, even if not close, friendships (e.g., in *Eva*, 232, 235, 311), is used in instances of disdain, insult and confrontations, especially between persons of different social levels (e.g., in *Una peccatrice*, 56-57 and in *Eva*, 302-303).

2.4.8. As polite forms, both *voi* and *lei* are more or less equally favored and *ella* is not at all overlooked. These forms are used in order of familiarity — from the more distant *ella* to the more amicable *voi* — and they are also determined by the social level dealt with in each novel. In the world of aristocracy and diplomacy they range from *ella* to *voi* while with the lower social classes the range goes from *lei* to the much more predominant *voi*.

The solemn form *ella*, [16] rarely used in Southern Italy, [17] aside from appearing in the role of regard (67, 77, E.100, E.107, et al.), is also seldom used in denoting distance, hostility and irony (cf. *Eros*, pp. 91, 97). The return to the *voi* form, once the familiar relationship with *tu* has already been established, may denote scorn (e.g., in *Eva*, pp. 265-67), temporary cooling of feelings (e.g., in *Eva*, p. 266) and transitory shyness (e.g., in *Eros*, p. 35).

2.4.9. The author, with certain applications of the personal pronouns, comes closest to the general spoken norm. Some structures that appear for the first time in these pages will become quite current in his later works. This is true, for example, with the presence of weak and strong pronominal forms: "Che *m*'importa di Maddalena *a me*" (28), "Che ti ho fatto *io* per meritar*mi* questo?" (99), "per non far*ti* credere anche *a te* che sia un capriccio" (E.68), "uomo più nobile e generoso ch'*io m*'abbia conosciuto" (77), "Ma *a te* che *te ne* importa?" (E.52). The pleonastic use of the weak *mi* and the redundant presence of the adverbial pàrticles *ci, vi* and *ne* especially, used as pronominal forms, are also attributable to the spoken norm: "*m*'avrò la sua visita" (E.55), "non so quel che *m*'abbia" (151), "*m*'ero lasciati di molti addietro" (145), "*m*'ha l'aria

---

[16] See Battaglia-Pernicone, *Grammatica*, p. 254.
[17] See Trabalza-Allodoli, *La Grammatica*, p. 140.

di un rajà indiano" (E.90); "La mia matrigna (...) *ne ha* le sue buone ragioni" (139), "non *ci* ho colpa" (139, 140, 187, 259), "Giuditta avea regalato al babbo un bel berretto (...) per fargli*ene* una sorpresa (150), *Ci* ho il mio giornale da digerire" (E.19), "non *ci* ho nessun merito" (E.94), "*Ci* ho della musica nuova" (E.124), et al.

Here are examples where the proclitic pronominal forms are clear indications of the Florentine vernacular: "*La* sarebbe finita come tutte le altre" (19), "*gli* è pel mio bene" (139), "Pare che *la* sia davvero una bella musica" (149), "Ero dispettoso che *la* fosse così (294), "La signora Zucchi, che *la* pretendeva ad elegante di provincia" (E.28), "ma *le* son fantasie e passeranno" (E.102), "La bimba *gli* rese il bacio" (E.117),[18] "*La* sa, signora mia, che cotesto io lo chiamo amore bell'e buono?" (E.157), "Anche *te* ti sei fatta bella" (E.21), "E anche *te*, sai, ti vuol bene" (E.21).[19] On rare occasions the pronominal *lo* with *potere*, appears when *fare* is understood ("giacchè non *l*'ho potuto con opere di maggior lena"-21, "Non *lo* posso, non *lo* posso ..."-208). Once *me*, rather than the normal *mi*, precedes the indirect object *gli* ("*Me* gli avvicinai col cappello in mano"-291). In addition to these examples that deal primarily with the article as pronominal form, there are also some with the pleonastic *si*;[20] "il mio primo pensiero *si* è la contentezza di trovarmi in mezzo alla mia famiglia" (140), "Se non gridai *si* fu perchè mi mancò il respiro" (167).

2.4.10. The author takes a definitely conservative attitude with respect to the pronominal enclitic forms. Although they are very popular at this time,[21] but on a decline, Verga will tend to use them

---

[18] Here *gli* stands for *le*, since it refers to a woman. In Trabalza-Allodoli, op. cit., p. 137, an example of a similar exchange of pronominal forms is cited from Fucini's *Veglia dei Neri*. It is also stated the Manzoni was very careful, in his last edition of *I Promessi sposi*, not to exchange the two forms. Also: "Anche al posto di *le* si sente *gli* nell'uso parlato": Battaglia-Pernicone, p. 247.

[19] On the *tu, te* forms D'Ovidio states: "nel toscano familiare...si può sostituire, in posizione enfatica, il *te* al *tu*." He also adds: "nè per questo è accolto nella lingua scritta." In Trabalza-Allodoli, p. 139. See also Battaglia-Pernicone, p. 243.

[20] "è un idiotismo toscano che si dovrebbe evitare": Gabrielli, *Dizionario linguistico moderno* (Milano, 1969). For the literary character of the idiom, cf. F. Ageno, *Il verbo nell'italiano antico* (Milano-Napoli, 1964), pp. 149-152.

[21] See Migliorini, *Storia*, p. 634.

more and more, not only here but also in the period that follows.
In these novels the highest frequency is reached in *Eros* but this
is not to say that he has not been fond of them even before. Not
taking into consideration the tenses that still take the enclitic form
— second person imperative, gerund, participle and infinitive — the
most favored tense, but not by far the only one, is the imperfect:
*sembravami, sembrami, tenevasi, confondevansi, erasi, parevami,
volgevasi, affaccendavasi, avrebbemi, potrebbesi, trattavasi, irradi-
vasi, parvegli, dilatavasi, mordevasi, credevasi, piegossi,* and so on.
The very rare use of the enclitic *meco* and *seco*, although used
in the Tuscan countryside but not in Florence, [22] should also be
considered as an aspect of a conservative attitude: "condurti *meco*
al passeggio" (24), "la nobiltà di fingerla *meco*" (115), "lo condusse
seco in giardino" (E. 32), "recando *seco* le sue malsane abitudini"
(E.140-41).

2.4.11. The author is much given to the literary [23] relative
pronoun *cui,* used, most times, with the preposition and to introduce
a subordinate clause. There are two cases, however, that deserve
attention. As the rule follows, the dative *a* is most times omitted
before *cui.* Thus: "con quell'attitudine abbandonata *cui* ella sapeva
dare tutto" (48), "il mal capitato Nicola, *cui* (...) nessuno avea
badato" (58), "Sarà forse un cervellino strambo il mio, *cui* meglio
conviensi la quiete del chiostro" (150), "I miei sogni erotici non
erano mai scesi più giù di una duchessa, *cui* prestavo (...) tutti i
miei entusiasmi" (238), "della mia famiglia, *cui* non avevo rivolto il
pensiero" (286), "che solo il cuore sa mettere fuori, e *cui* solo lo
sguardo sa dare il significato" (300), "Erminia, *cui* rifioriva nuovamente la salute" (387), and so on; but also: "parlando all'uomo
a cui dava il braccio" (27), "il sorriso *a cui* aveva forzato il suo
labbro sdegnoso" (66), "come ringraziassi il mio buon Dio (...) *a
cui* si schiudeva l'anima mia" (152), "nella donna *a cui* sentiva
il bisogno di identificarsi" (E.156). In the case of the specificative
di cui, at the cost of making his structure sound antiquated and
sometimes heavy, the alternate form *def. art.* + *cui* + *noun* is never
found. It is invariably *di cui* + *art.* + *noun*: "da quella donna,

---

[22] See Trabalza-Allodoli, *La Grammatica,* p. 134.
[23] See Trabalza-Allodoli, p. 149; also Rohlfs, *Morfologia,* p. 192.

di cui il lusso, il corteggio, l'adulazione era l'atmosfera in cui viveva" (28), "prende un bagno *di cui i profumi* costano ciascun giorno otto o nove lire" (36), "le tende del verone, *di cui le inve-triate* erano aperte" (43), "un giovane alto e bruno, *di cui l'espres-sione* fredda" (66), "seguì lo zio, *di cui il viso* andava rannuvolan-dosi" (E.56), "*di cui le persiane* rimanevano ostinatamente chiuse" (E.68), "Quello uomo, *di cui il nome* correva sulle bocche di tutti" (E.90), et al. Practically non-existent are even slight deviations from this word-order: "la pace e la libertà *di cui ho* bisogno" (45), "stava dinanzi alla moglie, *di cui istintivamente* indovinava i dolori" (398-99).

2.4.12. Quale, preceded by the contracted preposition, is much more infrequent than *cui*: "da farla vivere in quel lusso *nel quale* vive" (30), "*della quale* so il nome soltanto" (37), "verso *della quale* si chinava sorridendo il biondo" (70), "e *dei quali* spargevo le foglie sulla carta" (101), "i fiori *dei quali* era sempre piena la giardiniera" (101), "*della quale* i tratti (...) *della quale* gli occhi (...) *della quale* infine le labbra s'aprivano anelanti" (123), "*con le quali* si celava il viso" (283).

2.4.13. Among the demonstrative pronouns, *costui* (-ei, -oro) and *colui* (-ei, -oro) are very much in the picture. As with the de-monstrative adjective *cotesto* (see 2.3.10), these pronouns are not necessarily used to insinuate any degree of physical nearness or distance from the speaker [24] (see, e.g., in pp. 30, 55, 325, 400, 406, E.50, E.73, etc.). In this sense they replace the more common *questo* and *quello* although, the reader does occasionally find: "es-clamò *questi*" (45), "disse *questi* aspramente" (44), "Quando *questa* gli parlava" (67), "*Questa* è campagna" (136). From time to time, *costui* and *colui* acquire negative or pejorative implications, such as hostility and rancour — here the distance they imply may be interpreted in a psychological sense — [25] (as, e.g., in pp. 75, 86, 113, 383), and at other times they are used for emphatic purposes [26] (as, e.g., in pp. 195, 358).

---

[24] See Fornaciari, *Sintassi*, p. 73.
[25] See Trabalza-Allodoli, p. 142; also Rohlfs, *Sintassi*, pp. 204-05, and Battaglia-Pernicone, p. 259.
[26] See Fornaciari, *Sintassi*, p. 73.

2.4.14. Between *quello* and *quel,* Verga tends to prefer the troncated and more archaic form, especially in the latter phase: "aveano riso francamente di *quel* ch'era stato di quella sciocchezza" (336-37), "e *quel* lì, guardatelo" (343), "Vi dirò *quel* che sono io" (348), "senza finire *quel* che stava dicendo" (373), "nascondeva gelosamente *quel* che soffriva" (395), "non sembrava più *quel* di prima" (396), "di *quel* delle grandi occasioni" (E.18), "non avrebbe potuto esprimere *quel* che provava" (E.109-10), "se non fossi *quel* che sono" (E.124), "Fai *quel* che vuoi" (E.140), "è il marchese *quel* laggiù che ci arriva dall'India" (E.143).

2.4.15. *Cotesto* (and *codesto*) is much less favored as pronoun than as adjective (see 2.3.10) but nonetheless used: "non mi avevano insegnato neanche *cotesto*" (147), "Anche *cotesto!*..." (188), "Da principio anche *cotesto* fa una certa paura" (252), "Che rumore è *cotesto?*" (E.9), "Perchè mi dite *cotesto, ora?*" (E.10), "Ti rammenti anche di *codesto?*" (E.22), "*Cotesta* è la teoria del frutto proibito" (E.127), "Perchè non fate voi *codesto?*" (E.149).

2.4.16. *Istesso, stesso* and *medesimo* all serve as pronominal strengthening forms or, to use Jespersen's term, as pronouns of identity. [27] With *istesso,* although still very popular with the Florentine dialect, [28] the author gives further indication of a conservative attitude, since the prosthetic *i* in front of the impure *s* was disappearing. [29]

2.4.16a. Often *stesso* and *istesso* are used interchangeably with the same words. Thus one finds "nel tempo *istesso*" (75, 121, 321, 365, 409, E.17) as well as "nel tempo *stesso*" (E.58); "al verone *istesso*" (93) and "allo stesso *verone*" (33); "al modo *istesso*" (E.53, E.139) as well as "al modo *stesso*" (E.17) and "allo *stesso* modo" (E.73). With terms denoting the time of day and with the word *giorno*: "il giorno *istesso*" (374) and "lo *stesso* giorno" (361); "nell'ora *istessa*" (82), "oggi *stesso*" (367), "la mattina *istessa*" (388), "domani *stesso*" (E.102), "la sera *istessa*" (103, 351, 357) and "la sera *stessa*" (E.85).

---

[27] *Essentials of English Grammar* (University, Alabama: Univ. of Alabama Press, 1964), p. 171.
[28] See Tommaseo-Bellini, *Dizionario della lingua italiana* (Torino, 1924); also Rohlfs, *Morfologia,* p. 210.
[29] See Migliorini, *Storia,* p. 702.

2.4.16b. As a general rule, each one of these forms appears in one set position in the word-order. *Istesso*, for example, almost invariably follows the noun: "colla sua felicità *istessa*" (20), "alla vita *istessa*" (53), "la contessa *istessa*" (78), "l'aria *istessa*" (89), "la pietà *istessa*" (111), "quest'amore *istesso*" (112, 128, E.155), "nel godimento *istesso*" (118), "il signor Nino *istesso*" (145), "nell' albergo *istesso*" (E.164), "Adele *istessa*" (E.174), et al. There are, however, few exceptions: "nell'*istesso* tenore" (20), "dalla sua *istessa* insolenza" (62), "questo *istesso* momento" (198), "al mio *istesso* amore" (99).

2.4.16c. *Stesso* is the only form used as strengthener of the tonic personal pronouns and, as might be expected, follows the pronoun: "Io *stesso*" (30, 177, 139, E.11), "sè *stesso*" (15, E.89, E.99), "me *stessa*" (137, 93), "ella *stessa*" (367, E.61, E.67), etc. Almost always, however, it antecedes nouns and adjectives: "colla *stessa* calma rassegnata" (284), "collo *stesso* sorriso" (296), "colle *stesse* febbri" (297), "quando lo *stesso* albero getterà la *stessa* ombra" (312), "la *stessa* suocera, (...) collo *stesso* fazzoletto" (360), "lo *stesso* giorno" (361), "il soffio dello *stesso* uragano" (399), "colla *stessa* languida indifferenza" (31), "colla *stessa* capricciosa volubilità" (49).

2.4.16d. The more literary *medesimo*, which appears with more consistency in the later phase of this period, is used very rarely — we have found only one case — to emphasize the personal pronoun: "perchè era imbarazzato egli *medesimo*" (303). It almost exclusively appears with nouns and precedes them: "la *medesima* cosa" (342), "i *medesimi* invitati, le *medesime* signore (...), i *medesimi* signori (...) la *medesima* sposina (...) e infine quel *medesimo* sposo" (359-60), "quei *medesimi* occhioni divoranti" (374), "quel *medesimo* impeto" (400), "*medesima* aria" (E.12), "col *medesimo* tono" (E.45), "colla *medesima* calma" (E.114), "quella *medesima* donnina" (E.164-65) et al. Manzoni, on the other hand, uses this form much more freely. [30]

---

[30] Rohlfs points out that Riccardo Folli, in comparing the 1825 version of *I Promessi sposi* with that of 1840, has noted that the *egli stesso* of the former edition is replaced in the latter by *lui medesimo*; *Morfologia*, p. 210.

2.4.17. Among the indefinite pronouns, somewhat peculiar is the use of *un* where *uno* is needed. This, however, occurs only a few times and mainly in the first novel. While its use may be primarily the result of stylistic affectation, it is quite possible to trace this phenomenon to the Sicilian dialect. [31] "tutti i pregi di costei non valgono *un* solo di Maddalena" (23), "Pietro aveva avuto uno sguardo, *un* solo, per lei" (63), "della sua bocca tremante che ne formavano *un* solo" (88), "Sotto *un* di quegli alberi" (307).

2.4.18. With the passing of time, the author becomes increasingly fonder of the literary form *non so che* (with some slight variations, at times) quite in vogue in Italy throughout the pre-romantic and Manzonian period but not afterwards. [32] In these novels, seldom does this phrase appear in the earlier ones but it acquires predominance in *Eros*. The preference that Verga shows for this structure might find an ally not so much in the "Manzonian" influence but more in the renewed interest that the French Naturalists especially showed in it. [33] As a marginal observation, it could be safely assumed, we believe, that the adoption of this form could be considered an indication of the naturalistic trend that is to follow in Verga. It should not be forgotten, in fact, that "Nedda" appeared prior to *Eros*. If not anything else, the adoption of this form should be interpreted primarily as a concordant literary feeling with some of the writers on the other side of the Alps. Here are some examples: "che andassi tentoni in cerca di *non so che*" (292), "dava *un che* di vaporoso" (E.19), "le sonagliere dei cavalli avevano un *non so che* di festoso" (E.44), "appena terminati *non so quali* lavori di *non so qual* commissione" (E.111), "un *non so che* di attonito" (E.115), "avessero dato *non so qual* (...) attrattiva al desiderio" (E.128), "per far *non so che* cosa" (E.132), "spirito da *non so quale* inquietitudine" (E.141), "presidentessa di *non so qual* congregazione" (E.144), "*non so quali* misteriose attrattive"

---

[31] Cf. Rohlfs, *Morfologia*, p. 233.

[32] See G. Natali, "Storia del 'non so che'," *L. N.*, XII (1951), 49: "Dopo Manzoni, cessa la voga del 'non so che'. Se ne troverà qualche esempio sporadico."

[33] The "rejuvenation of *je ne sais quoi* is quite common with the Naturalists." N. in Wartburg, *Problems and Methods in Linguistics,* trans. Joyce M. H. Reid (Oxford, 1969), p. 94.

(E.152), "Anche quel *non so che* di furtivo" (E.153), "chiedeva (...) perdono di *non so quali* sospetti" (E.160), "lo sentiva (...) a quel *non so che* d'impacciato" (172-73).

2.5.1. With the first person singular of the present indicative of *fare*, although *faccio* predominates, there are instances where *fo* is seen: "*fo* così perchè così fanno gli altri" (19), "Ti *fo* riflettere che non ho ancora fatto colazione" (31), "mi *fo* un dovere di rimetterlo" (71), "giacchè ti *fo* piangere" (277). With *essere*, the Tuscanized *son* is clearly preferred to the standard *sono*, both for the first person singular and for the third plural: "ci *son* dei casi" (126), "Ci *son* dei momenti" (149), "chè *son* molto triste" (152), "io non *son* cattiva" (154), "allorchè lo ascolto *son* felice" (159) et al.

2.5.2 The use of some forms of the imperfect or past descriptive is oscillatory at times. The standard forms prevail, although there are numerous archaic constructions. In the first person singular, for example, the *-a* ending is occasionally noticed: "(io) ti *credeva* sui digesti" (29), "confesso che (io) me *l'aspettava* pochissimo" (72), "come io ne *aveva* bisogno" (99), "io mi *sentiva* tutta turbata" (155), "Io *tremava* [but] *balbettavo* non so che cosa" (163), "Io non *osava* guardarlo" (167), "Se mi avessero detto che (io) *doveva* soffrire tanto" (177), "(io) *pensava* a quella nostra casetta" (185), "del resto (io) non *aveva* che un'idea confusa" (194), "Domenica (io) *era* in coro ad ascoltare la messa" (205), "io *pensava, pensava* (...) io *pensava* al fiorellino" (210), "non *poteva* fissarla senza sentirmi andare tutte le veni..." (213), "io non *aveva* in prospettiva che i galloni di tenente" (369), "Io *era* ritornato ai miei bagni" (374), "Io mi *trovava* presente" (378), "(io) Non *sapeva* d'amarlo... non me n'*era* accorta" (410), "io non vi *aveva* fatto l'insulto di diffidare di voi" (E.64).

With *avere*, the third person *avea*, usually in the role of auxiliary, is just as popular — if not more — as *aveva*. By way of analogy perhaps, other syncopated forms are often found next to the standard ones: *vedea* (393 et al.), *volea* (371), *dovea* (27, E.10, E.129, E.135, et al.), *volgea* (E.177), *sapea* (27), *vivea* (91) and so on.

2.5.3. In the past absolutes, first and third person, the *-etti*
ending is less frequent than the stronger ending: "*insistè* Raimondo" (30), "il solo orecchio di Pietro *potè* distinguere" (39), "*perdè*
la pazienza" (39), "non *potei* dormire" (169), "*perdei* la testa" (277),
"non *potei* chiudere occhio" (289), "*temei* sul serio" (313), "non
potei dormire" (315), "se ne *diede* per intesa" (343), "*diede* (…)
la sua approvazione" (412), "*insistè* con un sorriso stentato" (E.52),
"si *diede* a tremare" (E.67), "*insistè* la mascherina" (E.71) et al.
Periodically, however, the weaker form is noticed: "*perdette* la
testa" (343), "*perdetti* (…) la testa" (350), "i suoi lineamenti *per-
dettero* le loro (…) alterazioni" (126). The strong *-si* ending is also
favored, in the first person, to the *-ii* ending: "quello che *soffersi*
in quel punto" (104), "che *benedissi* altra volta" (152), "che *soffersi* lassù" (184), "gli *offersi* un sigaro" (320), et al.

2.5.4. The archaic epenthetic *e* is occasionally found in the
first three persons of the future of *andare,* even though the syncopated forms are much more evident: "*anderà* superba un giorno
dell'amore di Pietro Brusio!" (63), "*anderò* a Napoli" (64), "Vi
anderò soltanto a condizione che ci venga anche tu" (97), "non
anderai più in convento" (153).

2.5.5. Without fail, the third person plural of the present
subjunctive *of essere* is *sieno* and never *siano*: "Quali novità vuoi
che ci *sieno*?" (29). "Credi che *sieno* marito e moglie?" (32),
"sembra che *sieno* stati più d'uno" (38), "ci pare che *sieno* nostri
amici da vent'anni" (146), "Mi pare che tutti gli occhi *sieno* fissi
su di me" (157), "mi pare che *sieno* diventati parte di me" (172-73),
"quali *sieno* i giorni di sereno" (237), "i giorni *sieno* contati" (328),
"pur troppo temo *sieno* inutili" (E.129). Double forms are found,
especially at the beginning of this period, for the second person of
the present subjunctive of *avere* and for the second and third of
essere. Abbi and *sii,* in other words, do have a brief existence:
"credo che tu *abbi* ragione" (18), "Credo che tu *abbi* ragione almeno per metà" (21), "non so quello che tu *abbi* stasera" (100),
"Non so più a qual numero *sii* …" (37), "come son contenta che
tu *sii* stato lì" (272). Most times, however, *abbia* and *sia* are used.

2.5.6. With the agreement of the past participles with *avere*
as auxiliary, the norm followed seems to be that if the emphasis is

placed on the object, the participle will agree with it. Otherwise, the participle will retain its neuter form. Thus we see: "giammai la Marina (...) *avea offerto* una riunione più bella" (28), "anch' egli *avea provato* tutta la lotta di quella disperata passione" (107), "*abbiamo fatto* una bella passeggiata" (143), "*ho analizzato* tutta me stessa" (154), "Per vivere alla meglio *avevo accettato* una delle più umili occupazioni" (281) et al. Also: "quelle che *avea fatta* la domanda" (77), "perchè *ho perduta* la mamma" (134), "coteste benedizioni che il Signore *ha date* a tutti" (135), "*hai conosciuta* quella russa?" (363), "Quando il dottore *ebbe finita* la sua narrazione" (364), "il dottore *avea raccontata* la storia della sua ammalata" (372), etc. However, the author oscillates in his handling of the past participle (with *avere*) when preceded by *mi*. With *mi* as direct object pronoun, there are times when the participle does not agree as it should — in gender with the person to whom *mi* refers: "Son morta! (...) *m'hanno disteso* sul cataletto, *m'hanno coperto* del drappo mortuario" (192-93), "*Mi hanno abbracciato*" (183), "Perchè tutti *mi avete abbandonato*, Marianna?" (197). In all these examples, the object is feminine. More often, however, the more accepted structure is used: "quando egli *mi amava* (...) *mi avrebbe pregata* di non uscire" (109), "*M'avevano abbigliata* da sposa (...) fui contenta per lui che *mi avrebbe veduta* così" (193), "perchè *mi avete abbandonata!*" (210), "Quando *mi avete abbandonata* per Velleda" (E.147). A similar flexible situation exists with *mi* as indirect object pronoun: "*mi aveva rovesciata* addosso quella narrazione" (300), "la stessa donna *mi avea fatta* sì strana impressione al teatro" (374), and also "lo troverei brutto perchè *mi ha rubato* la mia Erminia" (386). In one instance, for no obvious reason, we find "*L'ha udito* dunque?" (16) where the pronoun refers to the feminine *esclamazione*.

Not missing, among the participles, are also some double forms. *Visto*, for example, alternates with *veduto* ("Anch'io l'ho *visto*" -191, "Ho *veduto* Giuditta così bella" -191), and *perso* with *perduto*. On the other hand, while the various forms of the synonymous *fissare*, *fisare* and *affissare* are used only *fissato* is adopted — as rarely as it may appear as such — as a past participle: "L'occhialetto di Pietro stava quasi sempre *fissato* su quella loggia" (40).

2.5.7. On occasions, the pronominal form is added to verbs such as *tacere, morire* and *passare*. These cases, aside from the stylistic function of accentuating the subject's action,[34] also reflect a form of italianized Sicilian:[35] "Egli *si tacque*" (122, 237), "E *si tacque* nuovamente" (248), "e *si tacquero*" (E.26), "anche il pianoforte *si tacque*" (E.59), "questa povera donna *si muore* qui" (191), "quella poveretta *si muore* ..." (380), "Non ha cuore per comprendere quello che *si passa* nel mio" (106), "Tutta la mia vita *si passa* così (332-33).

2.5.8. If, on the one hand, the author is quite liberal with the "forma riflessiva apparente,"[36] (see, e.g., examples with *mi* in sec. 2.4.9), it is also true, at other times, that the reflexive particle *si* does not appear where expected: "esclamò Pietro *fatto* pensieroso" (38), "Un giorno era uscito prima ch'io *fossi* levata" (102), "Ella non rispose, e *voltò* indietro per ritornare" (E.135), "Gemmati avea perdonato quei torti (...) con una di quelle strette di mano che *armonizzavano* col suo viso aperto e leale" (E.163).

2.5.9. To the Sicilian norm might be attributed a couple of instances where *avere* appears instead of the correct *essere*:[37] "Dio mio ... vi *ha* una donna più sciagurata di me" (159), "e tu sai che la tua relazione con quella signora che tu sai comincia ad annoiarti, e che *ha durato* troppo" (363).

2.6.1. Up to this point the verb has been considered primarily in its morphological dimension. Since, as Guiraud well puts it, "le temps est... l'expression des sentiments du sujet parlant de sa vision, de ses relations intimes avec le sujet du récit,"[38] let us now turn our attention to the implementation of the various tenses or, to put it in another way, to the functional "aspects" that some of the more conspicuous tenses assume, partly because of the author's background but primarily because of his specific stylistic intentions.

---

[34] See Battaglia-Pernicone, p. 278. For the application of this phenomenon in archaic Italian and in classics, see F. Ageno, *Il verbo nell'italiano antico*, pp. 140-41 and 145-46.

[35] See A. Leone, "Caratteristiche," p. 91.

[36] Battaglia-Pernicone, p. 277. See also F. Ageno, op. cit., pp. 132-158.

[37] Cf. Rohlfs, *Sintassi*, p. 125.

[38] *Essais de stylistique* (Paris, 1969), p. 149.

2.6.2a. Usually the present indicative functions within the range of the narrative norm. As expected, it appears primarily in the dialogue and it is also the dominant tense of the epistolary narrative, [39] as seen in the second part of *Una peccatrice* and in *Storia di una capinera.* Occasionally it is also used in the atemporal sense of denoting a personal or common opinion free of any temporal duration. [40] Such is the case, for example, with the proverbs coined by the characters: "*Fo* così perchè così *fanno* gli altri" (19), "Fumo di gloria non *vale* fumo di pipa" (21), "Amor di donna (...) non *dura* più di cenere di carta, o biglietto amoroso ... o sigaro regalia" (21).

2.6.2b. In some constructions the present takes the place that is usually reserved for the past tense and particularly for the imperfect in the narrative. Since this is only noticed in the first pages of *Una peccatrice,* one might think that the author was only experimenting with this device. Its brief duration might very well indicate its limited success. At times the present is used with physiognomic descriptions:

> Pietro Brusio (...) *è,* come abbiamo accennato, un giovanotto alto, di circa 25 anni; *ha* i capelli assai radi (...). *È* un giovane quale se ne incontrano molti in Sicilia (...) *passa* colla maggior facilità dall'estrema confidenza nella sua *stella* (...) allo scoraggiamento massimo.

> Il compagno che gli passeggiava allato *è* molto più piccolo (...).

> Raimondo, Il biondo, *ha* però il merito di essere come il compimento del carattere infiammabile (...) del suo amico. Egli non *ha* la superiorità d'ingegno di lui, ma molta maturità di giudizio, *ciò* che lo *fa* ragionare calmo ed assennato (...) poichè Raimondo *ha* la voce dolce (...) sembra infine che l'ardente carattere dell'amico suo subisca a sua volta l'influenza della pacata indole di lui (...).

---

[39] See Guiraud, *Essais de stylistique* (Paris, 1969), p. 145. The epistolary narrative may also be considered in its overall picture as a direct discourse.
[40] See Fornaciari, *Sintassi,* p. 170; also G. Herczeg, "Su alcuni usi del presente," *L. N.,* XXIII (1962), 109.

Entrambi *appartengono* a due buone famiglie di Siracusa. Raimondo *è* già laureato in medicina (...) e Pietro *studia* legge per studiare qualche cosa ... (all above examples found in pp. 16-18.)

2.6.2c. The present, in *Una peccatrice,* is also used in instances where the author finds it necessary to suggest to the reader the background of an event about to unfold. This technique tends, as a result, to reduce itself to a function very similar to that of stage directions: [41]

Cinque giorni dopo (...) noi *incontriamo* i due amici che *passeggiano* (...) sotto gli alberi del *Rinazzo*: (18)

Venti giorni *sono* scorsi da quallo in cui incontrammo i due amici al *Rinazzo. Siamo* nei lunghi giorni del giugno. Pietro *studia* assiduamente da mattina a sera le sue tesi, poiché si *approssimano* gli esami; ed *esce* assai di rado. (25)

Siamo al Giovedì Grasso (...). Tutti mascherati in modo poveramente e orribilmente grottesco, *vanno* al Teatro a farvi pompa del cinismo del vizio (...) *occupano* la galleria, ove *mangiano, bevono, contendono* ed *urlano* (...). Dopo la recita *aspettano* l'apertura del ballo mascherato per lanciarsi (...) per mischiarsi a quella società elegante che non *sentonsi* in diritto d'avvicinare coi loro cenci. (60).

Parecchie settimane dopo, in Napoli, ad una delle serate che dava il barone di Monterosso, noi *ritroviamo* Narcisa ... (64).

Although Verga may have originally chosen to adopt this tense because of its relatively far-reaching limits and atemporal function [42] — as the examples in sec. 2.6.2b. indicate — or because of its ability to express in a more direct and vivid way the impression of past facts, [43] he soon discovers that this technical venture can have its

---

[41] With respect to stage directions, a similar observation has been made by M. Guglielmetti in his *Struttura e sintassi del romanzo italiano del primo Novecento* (Milano, 1964), p. 72, in regard to some aspects of Pirandello's prose.

[42] See Guiraud, p. 144: "Le présent étendu convient au portrait, à la description."

[43] See Guillame, *Temps et verbe* (Paris, 1929), p. 60.

shortcomings when applied to a genre such as the novel that traditionally has not been too congenial to it. By applying the present the narrator actually steps outside of the narration thus upsetting its natural flow.

2.6.3. In his excellent study, Weinrich echoes Brunetière's [44] and Meillet's [45] beliefs when he states that the Naturalistic writers of the 19th Century are not only interested in simply narrating a story but "en medida cresciente van arrogándose la tarea de informar al mismo tiempo con fidelidad científica (. . .) sobre la situación de la época." [46] In order best to achieve this the writers made generous use of the imperfect, a tense that, because of its descriptive nature, best lent itself to the description of such scientific-like information. Even if there are, during this period, certain factors that might tend to devalue somewhat Verga's "naturalistic" intentions, it cannot be denied, especially in view of his mature works, that he was well headed in this direction. The imperfect, although always a secondary tense—a tense, that is, that always functions as auxiliary to the dominant tense of the narrative—, [47] keeps on gaining not only superiority in the number of times it occurs but also, through the several ways in which it is utilized, a more unique stylistic prominence. Let us look, in the sections that follow, at its various functions.

2.6.3a. The imperfect tends to become the steady companion of certain adverbial forms and conjunctions. Syntagms such as *di tratto in tratto, di tanto in tanto, di quando in quando* appear almost exclusively with the imperfect (for example, see pages listed in sec. 2.7.1) while with conjunctions such as *allorchè* and *allorquando* the presence of this tense becomes somewhat less consistent but nevertheless noticeable (see examples in sects. 2.9.1 and 2.9.2).

2.6.3b. In addition to describing actions of a certain duration and continuity in the past, [48] the imperfect is also used in a "static"

---

[44] *Le roman naturaliste* (1881), p. 84.
[45] *Linguistique historique et linguistique générale* (Paris, 1921), p. 151.
[46] *Estructura y función de los tiempos en el lenguaje,* trans. F. Latorre (Madrid, 1968), p. 216.
[47] Cf. Weinrich, p. 208.
[48] See Fornaciari, *Sintassi,* p. 174.

sense or, to use Lerch's term, as the *imparfait pittoresque*. [49] It helps
in focusing on a scene of nature or on an interior setting and, just
like a snap shot, [50] the scene is immobilized in front of the reader's
eye and it is isolated from what comes before and after it:

> I viali *erano* affollatissimi; la musica *eseguiva* le più ap-
> passionate melodie di Bellini e di Verdi; un bel lume *si*
> *mischiava* alle vivide fiammelle dei lampioncini (...) che
> illuminavano i viali. (26)

> Per giungere al salotto si *attraversava* una piccola serra a
> cristalli, che *occupava* uno dei lati di una terrazza assai
> vasta (...). Quella specie di stufa (...) *circoscriveva* come
> in un'atmosfera separata dalla città clamorosa, il salotto ed
> il gabinetto da studio che vi *era* contiguo. (82)

> Il salotto *era* dobbato con lusso (...). Le porte vetrate, che
> si aprivano sulla terrazza, *erano* nascoste (...) da persiane
> di pianticelle rampicanti; ciò (...) *faceva* penetrare nella
> sala quella mezza luce... (83)

> Il sole *tramontava* da un lato, mentre la luna *sorgeva* dall'
> altro: alle due estremità due crepuscoli diversi, le nevi
> dell'Etna che *sembravano* di fuoco, qualche nuvoletta tras-
> parente che *viaggiava* per l'azzurro del firmamento (...)
> laggiù il mare che *s'inargentava* ai primi raggi della luna...
> (144)

> Il cielo *era* azzurro, il mare risplendente, *spirava* un'aria
> imbalsamata di fragranza che *faceva* sollevare il mio po-
> vero petto tanto malato... (210)

> La notte *era* tiepida e rischiarata da un bel lume di luna.
> *Sentivo* accanto a me quel respiro lievissimo come quello
> di una bambina... (247)

> Le camera *era* piccola, ed imbottita di seta bianca (...).
> In un canto *c'era* un letto tutto velato di trine (...). *C'era*
> un profumo singolare in quella camera (...). *C'erano* in
> tutti gli angoli quei piccoli oggetti che luccicano (...). *C'e-*
> *rano* negli specchi come il riflesso di chiome bionde... (259)

---

[49] "Das Imperfektum als Austruck der lebhaften Vorstellung," *Zeitschrift
für romanische Philologie*, 42 (1922), 311-331; cf. Weinrich, p. 215.
[50] Cf. Ronconi, "L'imperfetto descrittivo," *L. N.*, V (1943), 90-93, esp. 92.

Il villino abitato dalla contessa *era* nel viale Principe Amedeo, le sue finestre *chiudevano* da tre lati un giardinetto tascabile (...) ma *avevano* di faccia San Miniato (...). Le aiuole verdi del giardino (...) e quegli alberi (...) *facevano* un bel vedere sulla facciata nuova... (331)

I lumi *erano* spenti (...) nel corridoio che *metteva* alle stanze di Nata; l'uscio *era* socchiuso; (381)

The imperfect is also associated with this idea of "staticity" when the tense is used to describe the physical appearance and countenance of the various, but primarily female, characters: "*Vestiva* un semplice abito di tarlatane" (27), "Ella si *toglieva* soltanto a lunghi intervalli da quella positura per recarsi agli occhi un binocolo che *teneva* sui ginocchi e col quale *guardava* nella strada o verso la villa; ed indi (...) *lasciava* ricadere mollemente la testa sulla spalliera, e *sembrava* assorbirsi in quell'inerzia contemplativa che gli orientali cercano nell'oppio" (31), "Mia sorella *aveva* una veste e un cappellino color di rosa, *sembrava* felice" (189), "*Era* bionda, delicata, alquanto pallida (...) *aveva* gli occhi cerulei, grandi, a volte limpidi, quando non *saettavano* uno di quegli sguardi che riempiono le notti di acri sogni; *aveva* un sorriso che non si *poteva* definire sorriso di vergine in cui *lampeggiava* l'imagine di un bacio. Ecco che cosa *era* quella donna (...). L'ammirazione che ella *destava assumeva* la forma di un desiderio" (227), "Ella *aveva* una cuffietta assai modesta; alcune ciocche di biondi capelli le *scappavano* attraverso i nastri scoloriti; sul suo seno s'*incrociava* un leggiero scialletto; *aveva* le labbra pallide e le mani livide" (282-83), "Adele *era* magrina, delicata, pallidetta, così bianca che *sembrava* diafana, e che le più piccole vene *trasparivano* con vaga sfumatura azzurrina; *aveva* grand'occhi turchini (...) il vento, innamorato, modellava le vesti sul suo corpicino svelto e gentile" (E.17), et al.

2.6.3c. With *Eva*, the imperfect begins to acquire a new dimension that can be best understood by taking into account psychological and stylistic views. In this novel, whose central part consists of a first person flashback narration told by the protagonist, Enrico Lanti, there are instances where the imperfect takes the place, as one can judge from the context, of a more definite past tense. Recounting his first encounter with Eva, Pietro says: "Ci sorrise (...) riprese come una maschera il suo sorriso, e disparve. *Rimanevo* tristamente là dov'erano svanite le mie illusioni" (243). While the first sentence states a completed action in the past (as the past absolute indicates), the second describes Enrico's reaction. A more logical sequence of tenses would have required *rimasi* and not *rimanevo*. It becomes clear that this tense is used for purposes that go beyond the mere temporal function. As he narrates the story, Enrico is also reliving it; and when he touches upon those moments that still have for him a highly dramatic and emotional intensity, he would like to linger mentally on them for as long as he can. He knows that they are in the past never to be realized again. In our judgment, in this and similar cases, the imperfect is used to express a "naturale commozione di fronte ai fatti narrati." [51] Here, the definition of this tense is to be sought not so much in terms of its temporal concept but mainly in connection with the way the narrator perceives reality: [52] a reality discerned in the sense of "vision." [53] The imperfect, by suddenly imposing itself on the reader, awakens in him the sensation of a certain "abnormal" attitude on the part of the speaker who, by momentarily abandoning his logical point of view along which the past has been unfolding, ceases to make of the action the object of the "presentation." [54] Here are other examples from *Eva*:

> Apersi il biglietto e lessi (...). *Rimanevo* come sbalordito dalla sorpresa, leggendo e rileggendo quelle due o tre righe... (246)

> Stavolta partì davvero. *Rimanevo* estatico, come inchiodato dinanzi a quella porta, respirando l'aria fredda della notte a pieni polmoni... (253)

> Ella corse verso di me (...) e mi diede un bacio. E quand'io la *baciavo*, quand'io la *soffocavo* di carezze deliranti, ella *metteva* un piccolo grido: un grido pieno d'amore e di voluttà. (260)

> Allorchè *partivo*, sull'alba, ella mi chiamò, mi attirò sui guanciali, allacciandosi tenacemente al mio collo... (269)

---

[51] O. Degregorio, "L'abuso dell'imperfetto," *L. N.*, VII (1946), 70.
[52] See L. Mourin, "L'imperfetto indicativo," *L. N.*, XVII (1956), 87.
[53] *Ibid.*, 84.
[54] *Ibid.*, 85.

'Perchè me lo domandi? Non mi ami? Non ti amo? Non siamo felici?'
Ella *appoggiava* la testa sul cuscino, rivolta dalla mia parte, e mi *fissava* senza parlare, coi suoi grandi occhi pieni di lagrime. (269)

2.6.3d. Also present is the so-called "narrative imperfect," occasionally used in Italian literature by writers such as Foscolo, Leopardi and Manzoni.[55] With this technique, primarily of an intellectualistic and literary nature, the omniscient novelist (the author as opposed to the character), in addition to revealing his own sensitivities, mood and the various gradations of his intervention in the narrative, places in front of the reader not only the action and its development but also the attitude of the subject and the impression of other characters.[56] The most prominent example is found in *Tigre reale*:

> Poi l'indomani Giorgio la *incontrava* in un ballo, o la *vedeva* nel suo palchetto alla Pergola, scollacciata, coperta di pizzi (...); l'amico, il camerata del giorno innanzi *confondevasi* fra la folla che le faceva ressa attorno, ella lo *distingueva* appena con un mezzo sorriso, non gli *apparteneva* più, *rientrava* nella sua sfera a testa alta. Una volta, in mezzo ad un ballo fu colta dalla tosse...
>
> (343-44)

As for additional examples:

> 'Addio,' gli ripetè allorchè furono al cancello (...). Giorgio *rimaneva* mutolo (...); le *teneva* la mano, e la *stringeva* forte. (346)

> Alle parole del dottore *succedeva* un silenzio penoso. La signora Ruscaglia *piagnucolava* in un canto del canapè per conto suo (...); Erminia, seduta ai piedi del letto, covando cogli occhi il bambino, non si *muoveva*; (388)

> Egli (Alberto) rimase un istante sbalordito (...). Alberto non *diceva* una parola, e *rimaneva* come di sasso; (E.92)

---

[55] See Ronconi, 92.
[56] *Ibid.*, 93.

A poco a poco incominciarono a venire gli amici di casa e l'Armandi *presentava* il marchese Alberti come se fosse arrivato dall'Australia. (E.94)

Tutti si erano affrettati attorno al suo carniere ben pieno facendogli i mirallegro. Velleda sola *rimaneva* zitta. (E.51)

2.6.4a. Using a mathematical analogy, Fornaciari states that just as the present perfect is to the present, the past perfect is to the imperfect. The difference, however, between these last two related tenses is that while the former verb expresses a completed action the latter expresses an action still in its duration. With this in mind, it is almost to be foreseen that the increasing frequency of the imperfect also extends to the past perfect (or pluperfect). This tense begins to gain greater eminence from *Eva* on and, along with the past absolute, it functions as one of the dominant tenses of the narrative. Without clearly indicating the end of a process, [57] it is used primarily to introduce passages of usually ample duration that, sooner or later, lead to a culminating point. [58] Here are some illustrations showing how this tense introduces passages denoting a prolonged and at times unclearly defined period of time within or after which an important action is expected: "L'inverno *era ritornato,* e rigidissimo" (281), "Io *avevo vissuto* vent'anni in dieci mesi, e mi sentivo forte" (292), "L'inverno *era sopravvenuto,* grigio e triste" (327), "Verso quell'epoca ella *evea avuto* un capriccio per un saltimbanco" (342), "*Era passato* del tempo! Babbo La Ferlita *era morto*; Giorgio *avea preso* moglie; noi *eravamo invitati* per un'altra festa di famiglia" (359), "*Erano passate* due settimane; la primavera *era* alquanto *inoltrata*" (367), "Al cominciar della primavera la contessa Armandi *era partita*" (E.88), "*Erano trascorsi* parecchi anno, e Alberti *aveva ricominciato* a fare la vita di prima" (E.138), et al.

2.6.4b. It has already been noted that this tense shares its duties as dominant tense with the past absolute. In Verga's case, this situation is of particular interest since one would expect that because of his regional background the author would have favored

---

[57] See E. A. Llorach, *Estudios de gramática funcional del español* (Madrid, 1970), p. 83.
[58] See Trabalza-Allodoli, p. 210.

the latter tense. [59] Not only is this not the case but a closer look reveals that these two tenses, when present in the same thought, fulfill a specific psychological function. As a rule, the pluperfect, functioning more precisely as a "retropluperfect," [60] is used to narrate facts, seen in retrospect by the narrator and almost devoid of any emotional intensity. It is used, in other words, primarily for factual and objective statements. The past absolute, on the other hand, introduces and immediately precedes situations and incidents bearing higher degrees of emotional charge. The examples are many and they are more apparent when seen within their context. The following illustrations will help in making this point clearer:

> *Avevo incontrato* due volte quella donna (...). L'*avevo incontrata* due volte, e non mi *era sembrata* la stessa donna (...). (But) la *rividi* anche mascherata... (it is, in fact, with the masquerade party that the story begins). (227-29)

> Quelle due ore *avevano gettato* sul mio cuore il soffio ardente delle tempeste del passato (...). *Feci* mille pazzie per lei, la *cercai, implorai, piansi, passai* le notti sotto le sue finestre... (298)

> Rendona non *aveva potuto* fare la solita visita della sera (...) perchè *era stato chiamato* in tutta fretta a casa La Ferlita. Col cader del giorno il male del bambino *si era aggravato* ... a la difterite *si era manifestata* (...).
> Giorgio *arrivò* a casa che era prestissimo. La porta aperta a quell'ora insolita, i domestici affacendati, gli *misero* addosso un gran turbamento e lo *fecero* correre alla camera della moglie in grande agitazione (...). Giorgio si *avvicinò* al letto come non si reggesse bene sulle gambe; *interrogò* ansioso l'aspetto del bimbo che dormiva, poi *prese* con mano tremante la mano della moglie. (386-391)

> Alberto *passò* una notte orribile. *Aveva visto* (...) la donna che amava alla follia accasciata sul canapè, colla testa fra le mani — ella non *avea fatto* un passo verso di lui, non *avea messo* un grido — egli non *avea potuto* stendere le braccia per soccorrerla o per rapirla alla gelosia del suo

---

[59] In Migliorini-Leone, *Grammatica Italiana* (Firenze, 1963), p. 119, it is stated that the past absolute is used little in the North but overused in the South.

[60] William E. Bull, *Time, Tense and the Verb,* University of California Publications of Linguistics, 19 (Berkeley, 1960), p. 43.

rivale (...). Il domani *seppe* che marito e moglie *erano partiti* all'alba. (E.133)

Finalmente una sera piovosa (...) Alberto *ritornò* a Firenze, e *arrivò* a casa sua quasi all'improvviso.
Al suo annunzio Adele *s'era rizzata* di botto in piedi; tutto il sangue le *era corso* al viso e vedendolo rientrare *era ricaduta* tremante sulla poltrona... (E.175)

2.6.5. With the handling of the past absolute, the author's regional background enters into the picture, but it can be readily stated that Verga, concerned with detaching himself from his native norm, is usually very careful with the handling of this tense and there are very few instances where the presence of this verbal form may be associated with his Sicilian origin. It may be because of this "hypercautious" attitude, however, that this tense does stand out whenever its appearance reflects the regional norm.

2.6.5a. The past absolute is traceable to the Sicilian dialect — the few times that it is found — in the dialogue and in the direct discourse. It replaces the more accepted compound past tense, best suited for instances — such as these — where the time span within which the action is produced is still in relation to the present. [61] In *Una peccatrice,* for example, when Raimondo asks "Chi te lo dice?", Pietro answers: "Tutto (...) il modo stesso con cui *accolse* la tua esclamazione" (16). Later, to Raimondo's "Che c'è?" Pietro replies: "Cospetto!... la signora che *incontrammo* l'altra volta alla villa!" (21); just after Raimondo tells Pietro that "bisogna essere uomini!", the latter says: "Ben *dicesti*! bisogna essere uomini e non fanciulli!" (44). When Pietro and Raimondo arrive at a party they are greeted by the hostess with the following: "Vi *lasciaste* molto aspettare, signorini!" (34); and when Pietro confesses to Narcisa that he is no longer able to concentrate on his work: "*Tentai* di lavorare per adempiere in parte agli obblighi impostimi, ma ti confesso che nulla mi è riuscito" (104). In *Eva,* Enrico tells the author: "*Fummo* a scuola insieme" (232); and later, again: "Noi non *fummo* mai intimi" (309). When Enrico asks his father "Perchè mi lasci così spesso?" the latter replies: "*Accompagnai*

---

[61] Cf. Llorach, p. 43.

il dottore, figliuol mio..." (314). In the examples cited above, since all the speakers are Sicilian the presence of this form can be stylistically interpreted as a way of adhering to the Sicilian spoken norm. In *Eros,* however, this cannot be the case because the speakers are not from Sicily but from the North. At a secret rendevous, Velleda tells Alberto: "Io *venni* per dirvi che sono la figliuola del conte Manfredini!"; to this he counter-replies: "Io ci *venni* per dirvi che son pazzo di voi!" (E.64). In a dialogue between Adele and Alberto, to his "Perchè hai accondisceso..." she replies: "Non me lo *domandasti* tu?..." (E.33).

2.6.5b. The influence of the Sicilian norm may also be the cause of some occasional switch in the same thought, from the less remote tense to the perfect, or viceversa: "*Ho mandato* il domestico a cercarlo al teatro, e *ritornò* dicendo che il teatro era chiuso da un pezzo" (42), "*Feci* e *disfeci* venti volte le sue trecce, ed ogni volta non ne rimaneva soddisfatta (...). Allora *sono uscita* asciugandomi gli occhi" (164-65), "Oggi *ho passato* tutto il giorno a guardare la porta (...). Non *vollero* che io rimanessi a guardarla più a lungo" (216-17).

2.6.5c. At the beginning of this period the author conforms to the norm when he uses the past absolute to describe an action completed within a period prior to "today." [62] Thus, it is often found with *ieri* or with any other adverb of time denoting a more remote period: "Ieri *ebbi* la fortuna di raccogliere un mazzo" (71), "Poco tempo fa lo *rividi* in una festa" (86), "Ieri *volli* uscire con lui; *volli* fare una passeggiata in barca" (116), "Ieri l'altro (...) le *domandai* il permesso di abbracciarla" (140), "L'altra sera i signori Valentini *portarono* il loro *armonium*" (147), "Ieri l'altro *vidi* un' ombra alla finestra" (157), "Ieri *fu* il Natale" (174), "Ieri una farfalletta *venne* sui vetri" (196), "L'altra notte *tentai* strascinarmi sino al tavolino" (197), "Ieri (...) il buon dottore mi *permise* di uscire" (200), "Ieri sera mi *lasciasti* in tal modo!" (273).

Sometimes this form is also used to describe an action occurring within the "today" time span: "la mia matrigna stamane mi *chiamò* (...). Ella *ripigliò* con quella stessa cera che mi faceva

---

[62] See Fornaciari, *Sintassi,* p. 170.

male (...). Ed *accompagnò* queste poche parole con tale sguardo e tal suono di voce" (163-64). But it doesn't take long for the author to take a more flexible approach to these forms by using other past tenses: "come ieri sera *l'ho veduta*" (79), "Ieri verso il tramonto *abbiamo fatto* una bella passeggiata" (143), "Ieri *era andato* a Catania" (160), "Ieri l'altro *l'ho vista* a Firenze" (E.73), "Ci *ho dato* un'occhiata ieri stesso" (E.117), et al.

2.6.5d. As already seen in sec. 2.6.4a, aside from functioning as one of the dominant tenses of the narrative, the past absolute is often applied to both simple and paratactic constructions for the purpose of adding to the narration a rapidity in tempo. This technique, in addition and in relation to the role of the past absolute as an emotionally charged tense (see sec. 2.6.4b), not only suggests to the reader a rapid subsequence of events but also points to the emotional tension achieved by certain actions in response to a previous significant incident. In cases of the sort, this verbal form, by characterizing itself through a process of accumulation, plays an important part in giving to the narration that synoptic and condensed aspect [63] needed to illustrate such a rapidity. As an example, this is how Enrico Lanti narrates his actions just after Eva has left him:

> *Scrissi* ai miei genitori, *fumai* la mia pipa, *riordinai* tutti i miei utensili da dipingere (...). E allora *incominciai* una lotta più bassa, più accanita, più dolorosa...
> Mi *venne* in mente di giocare. Mi *ricordai* di tutte quelle storielle di guadagni enormi (...). *Salii* senza esitare le scale (...) *arrischiai* una lira (...). Poi *sentii* una gran calma improvvisa (...). *Scesi* le scale con passo fermo.
> Il giorno dopo *pensai* ch'era naturalissimo di andare a chiedere qualche cosa in prestito al solo amico che non mi voltasse ancora le spalle....
> Verso le sei mi *trovai* senza avvedermene dinanzi all' osteria dove solevo desinare....
> Verso sera le mie sofferenze *si fecero* insopportabili. *Uscii* come un pazzo. Mi *trascinai* dinanzi a tutti i caffè (...). Poi, tutto a un tratto mi *trovai* abbietto.... *Vidi* uscire una coppia di giovani eleganti (...). Me gli *avvicinai* col cappello in mano e gli *dissi*: "Ho fame." (286-291)

---

[63] See Weinrich, p. 214; also G. Herczeg, *Lo stile nominale in italiano* (Firenze, 1967), pp. 113-14.

Soon thereafter the rapidity of this narration is confirmed by the author himself: "Egli mi aveva rovesciata addosso quella narrazione come una valanga, tutta di un fiato, quasi fosse stato uno sfogo supremo e disperato" (300).

2.6.6. Among the infinitive verbal forms, the gerund is of distinct prominence. This form, of extreme popularity with the Italian writers of the past,[64] will always remain so dear to Verga that, in his mature works, not only will it be used with reference to the subject but also to other members of the proposition.[65]

2.6.6a. Only once does the gerund appear in these pages in its archaic form of adverbial complement introduced by *in*: "Ma se tu fossi destinato ad amare quella donna, che non hai veduto che due volte, *in passando*?..." (25).[66] Equally rare is the presence of this form in clauses expressive of concession: "Gemmati l'aveva assistita come sorella o come figlia, e, *pur dissimulando* la gravità del male, aveva insistito perchè non fosse informato Alberto" (E.174).

2.6.6b. While Verga is very careful not to show his Southern tendencies with circumlocutions such as *stare + gerund,* less careful is he with *andare + gerund,* also indicative, this form, of the South,[67] and used in the progressive concept: "in quanto a quello che mi *vai cantando* di accalappiamenti e di poverette" (18), "Non è poi quella maraviglia che mi *vai cantando*..." (22), "I palchetti si *andavano popolando* di belle signore" (239).

2.6.6c. Occasionally the gerund is preceded by the adverb *così*: "*Così dicendo* gli scosse brevemente la mano" (330), "*Così*

---

[64] See Battaglia-Pernicone, p. 380.

[65] Migliorini, *Storia,* p. 710, quotes one example from *Mastro-don Gesualdo*: "Rosaria ... vide la padrona in uno stato spaventevole, *frugando* nei cassetti e negli armadi."

[66] Although Rohlfs, *Sintassi,* pp. 107-8, points out that this form is also popular in the vernacular Tuscan, we are more inclined to believe, because of its appearance only in the early part of this period, that its presence can be attributed more to its archaic and literary use. Not to be overlooked either is the possibility of a close copy of the French *en passant.*

[67] See Rohlfs, *Sintassi,* pp. 108-9.

dicendo andava diritta pel viale" (346), *"Così attraversando* le sale a braccetto" (355). Too self-conscious, perhaps, of *così* + *gerund* of *dire,* the author will also entertain, but briefly, the awkward structure *così* + *infinitive:* "In *così dire* si mise a tossire di nuovo" (347).

2.6.6d. Most unique and distinctive is the gerund accompanied by the conjunction *come* and, less often, *quasi* (see examples in sec. 2.9.8b). These constructions will prevail throughout this period, even if with decreasing frequency.

2.6.6e. Most times, however, the gerund appears in the implicit subordinate clause, showing causal or temporal value. In these instances it replaces *mentre* + *the finite indicative* tenses of the *preposition* + *article* + *infinitive:* "Raimondo Angiolini *entrando* in chiesa venne a stringerci la mano" (10), "Dal canto mio non ho fatto che cordinare i fatti, *cambiando* i nomi qualche volta ed anche *contentandomi* di accennare le iniziali (...) *rapportandomi* spesso alla nuda narrazione di Angiolini (...) *aggiungendovi* del mio soltanto la tinta uniforme" (13), "diceva il biondo, *guardando* l'amico negli occhi in aria di malizia" (18), *"Vedendo* quel sangue, udendo quel pigolare...io piansi" (141), *"fissandomi* di un'occhiata che sembrava mi penetrasse" (163), "Rimanevo sbalordito dalla sorpresa, *leggendo* e *rileggendo* quelle due o tre righe, *sentendomi* serpeggiare fiamme" (246), *"ridendo* come una bambina" (255), *"prendendogli* le mani nuovamente, gli disse" (347), *"Attraversando* il vestibolo del teatro, Giorgio si scusò di non essere in giubba" (351), *"rivolgendo* ad Alberti la parola solamente quel po' ch'era necessario" (E.73), *"Vedendomi,* ella mi riconobbe subito" (E.101), et al.

2.7.1. A noticeable degree of flexibility is shown in the use of the various adverbs. Verga resorts to forms identifiable with the spoken — and to the Sicilian in particular — as well as with the literary and sometimes archaic norm.

Verga's desire of adopting himself to the spoken norm is clearly indicated by the constantly growing number of reduplicated or germinal adverbial forms: *leggero leggero* (45), *stretto stretto* (162), *chete chete* (166), *lento lento* (365, 384, E.184), *zitte zitte* (386, 397,

403), *forte forte* (142), *tanto tanto* (410), *lontano lontano* (136, 312, 160), *grado grado* (144), *secco secco* (236), *pian pianino* (170, 171), *tratto tratto* (395), *seria seria* (E.127, E.145, E. 178), *mogia mogia* (E.120), *asciutto asciutto* (E.23, E.73), *rossa rossa* (E.27), *allora allora* (E.66), et al. Equally popular are the adverbial phrases such as *di tanto in tanto* (145, 170, 190, 333, 374, 384, 390, 397, 406, E.28, E.31, E.39, E.45, E.82, et al.), *di quando in quando* (301, 312, 347, 407, E.130, E.133), *a poco a poco* (301, 353, 361, 366, E.94, E.124, et al.), *(a) faccia a faccia* (326, 328, 379, E.132, E.143), *di giorno in giorno* (400), *di tratto in tratto* (160, 381, 393, et al.), *ad una ad una* (160, 409).

2.7.2. With the adverbs of time the literary and more popular *ora* is a clear favorite over *adesso* and very much in evidence is also the archaic and literary [68] *poscia*, strongly preferred to the more conventional *poi* and *dopo poco*: "*poscia* si fece al verone" (45), "domandai *poscia*, come non accorgendomene" (114), "mi domandò *poscia*" (165), "*poscia* con un sorriso tutto gaio" (250), "*Poscia* quei sorrisi, quegli occhi" (252), "*Poscia* tutti i sigari si spensero" (305); see also pp. 308, 346, 352, 381, E.73, E.79, et al. The literary *indi*, usually followed by the past absolute, is also an occasional substitute for *poi* and *quindi*: "*indi* (...) lasciava ricadere mollemente la testa" (31), "*indi* rimase alcuni minuti in silenzio" (25), "*indi* si mette al pianoforte, o al verone" (36), "*indi* (...) ella si volse un istante verso il conte" (39), "*indi* lasciò quasi cadere (...) il binocolo" (41). "*Indi*: quando il vento avrà fatto stormire le foglie" (161), "*Indi* la porta si rinchiuse" (189), "*indi* le si avvicinò," (E.103), et al.

2.7.3. Quite popular throughout this period, and appearing in its various orthographic forms, is the adverb *di già*, a poor second to *digià* and, even more, to the highly unusual *diggià*: [69] "*Diggià*!... il giorno vien presto al presente!" (46), "*Digià*!" (252), "temete *digià* di mancare!" (253), "Si vedeva *digià* il cadavere" (308), "sbatteva *digià* la sua livida ala" (308), "*digià* per tre quarti cadavere" (310), "Te ne vai *digià*?" (314), "col piede *di(g)già*

---

[68] See Trabalza-Allodoli, p. 244; also Battaglia-Pernicone, p. 399.
[69] The form *diggià* does not appear in any of the sources that we have consulted. The Tommaseo-Bellini dictionary registers only *di già* and *digià*.

(*g* inserted by editor) nella fossa" (301), "essa lo conosce *diggià*" (324), "ha *diggià* i capelli" (360), "fossimo *diggià* arrivati" (379), "È giorno *diggià?*" (385), "siamo *di già* a questi ferri?" (E.31), "ti sei innamorato *diggià* della mia mano?" (E.72), "Sei tornata... *diggià!*" (E.172), et al.

2.7.4. A considerable amount of wavering also takes place with other forms of adverbs of time. *Iersera* and *ier l'altro*, forms that are both literary and popular with the spoken Tuscan [70] ("*Iersera* so che avete fatto una grossa perdita" -E.118, "sei venuto a cercarmi *iersera*" -E.119, "Frattanto *ieri l'altro* [...] vidi un'ombra" -157, "mi ha chiesto di lei *ier l'altro*" -324, "*Ieri l'altro* l'ho vista a Firenze" -E.73), share the spotlight with other forms such ıs *ieri a sera* ("siamo qui da *ieri a sera*" -180) and *l'altro ieri* ("*L'altro ieri* [...] le domandai il permesso di abbracciarla" -140). *L'indomani,* found mostly in the first four novels, (16, 71, 112, 343, 402, 406) is replaced in *Eros* by *il domani* (see, i.e., pp. 23, 50, 88, 133, 172, 178). Next to the literary *doman l'altro* (331, E.93), one also finds the more Sicilian inspired *posdomani* (119). More conspicuous is the anomalous *stassera,* which appears consistently in the first pages of *Una peccatrice* (28, 29, 37, 49), but is thereafter replaced by the standard *stasera* (73, 354, 362, E.107, E.160, E.178).

2.7.5. Among the adverbs of place the less popular and more poetic *ove* is often found next to the more conventional *dove*. While the latter is used mainly with questions ("*Dov'è* Pietro? *Dov'è* mio figlio [...] ? [...] *Dove* la laciaste voi? ..." -42), the former is the heavy favorite in the narration and it often takes the place of the *preposition + definite article + relative pronoun*: "verso la casa *ove* abitava la contessa" (42), "nel salire le scale della casa *ove* andavamo" (100), "Alla festa, *ove* l'accompagnai" (101), "*ove* avea sciolto del sapone" (125), "*ove* per andare all'abitazione più vicina bisogna correre (...) *ove* non si ode" (136), "*ove* vi ostinaste in questa follìa" (299), "*ove* la morte sbatteva digià la sua livida ala" (308), et al.

---

[70] See Rohlfs, *Sintassi,* p. 266.

2.7.6. *Costà* and *colà,* rapidly falling into disuse and, according to Leone, virtually unknown in Sicily,[71] are occasionally used in place of the more common *quì, qua, lì* and *là*: "mi hanno lasciato morir *colà,* sola" (178), "*Colà* si sapeva sempre ove cercare una persona" (182), "*Colà* egli si riposava" (399), "siete ancora *costà*?" (E.22), "O che fa lei *costà*" (E.23), "Ti vedrò *colà*" (E.71), "Tutti dicevano *colà* che ci ritornerà" (E.102), "*costà* (...) ci dev' essere una certa mia villetta" (E.102), "Mi stabilirò *colà*" (E.180).

2.7.7. Not uncommon is the literary *onde,* used exclusively with the implicit infinitive as an alternative to the final *per* + *infinitive*: "andò ad origliare dietro la bussola della camera di sua madre, *onde* vedere se dormiva" (45-46), "*onde* stordire tutto quello che sentiva d'ignobile" (58), "*onde* prevenire il giovane" (77), "che facessi di tutto *onde* venire ad un accomodamento" (79), "*onde* vivere soltanto per questa vita" (90), "*onde* fissarsi ancora su Pietro" (124), "*onde* inginocchiarmi ai piedi del crocifisso" (160), "*onde* fare entrare quell'aria imbalsamata" (141), "*onde* vedere la mia finestra (...) *onde* cercare (...) il luogo" (181), "*onde* delirare per quella donna" (310), "*onde* aver agio di menar il can per l'aia" (E.34), "*onde* abbeverarsi di tutte quelle vergini sensazioni" (E.153). The only time that *onde* is not followed by the infinitive is when it is followed by the negative *non*: "*onde non dia* più occasione ad attendermi domani" (45).

2.7.8. Among the affirmative adverbs, *anche* is a clear favorite over *pure* and it is very often used in structures that reflect the spoken norm, the Tuscan in particular. *Anche,* practically unknown in the South but the only form known in Tuscany,[72] is used to accompany the pleonastic — but useful, for emphatic reasons — personal pronoun that refers to the subject. Here are some illustrations: "Il signor Nino *anch*'egli ha un bel cane" (144), "Gigi piangeva *anche* lui" (201), "la folla delle maschere urlava *anch*'essa" (301), "Erminia s'era fatta pallida *anch*'essa" (413), "L'Armandi partiva *anch*'essa pei bagni" (E.99), "Ella s'era alzata *anche* lei"

---

[71] "Di alcune caratteristiche dell'Italiano di Sicilia," *L. N.,* XX (1959), 85-93.
[72] See Rohlfs, *Sintassi,* p. 260.

(E.129), "Adele s'era fatta seria *anch*'essa" (E.153). On one occasion *neppur,* associated to *pure,* is used with this type of structure and the reason may be attributed, as the example will illustrate, to the wish of not wanting to be repetitive: "Erminia non aveva dormito *neppur* essa; ... sembrava inquieta *anche* lei" (405).

2.7.9. The negative reinforced adverbial form *giammai* is a heavy favorite throughout this period (9, 30, 40, 60, 110, 162, 219, 269, 279, 289, 295, 312, 358, 359, E.68, E.71, E.89, E.161, et al.). *Mai,* on the other hand, remains always a poor second although it is used with more frequency in the later phase of this period (249, 343, 358, et al.).

2.7.10. The Tuscan and Florentine form *punto,* [73] used to emphasize a negative statement, also has an occasional appearance. At times it appears without any other negative particle ("L'ami molto? *'Punto'* " -296, "Fa molto freddo oggi? - *Punto*: È una bellissima giornata" -335) but most times it does: "volete che mi dia a voi (...) senza amarvi *punto*?" (348), "ma di naso sembra invece che non ne abbia *punto*" (360), "non sembra *punto* allegro!" (E.30), "non è *punto* allegro stasera!" (E.100), "che non stimava *punto*" (E.173).

2.7.11. Among the adverbs of manner, the switch that takes place towards the middle of this period between the archaic *sì* and the more conventional *così* is noticeable. While the former prevails from the days of *I carbonari della montagna* up to *Storia di una capinera,* the latter takes over almost completely from then on. Neither of these forms is used in its strict accordance with the norm, as implied by Fornaciari. *Così,* in other words, does not necessarily precede an adjective or another adverb while *sì* is not necessarily used to bring forth a relation between two thoughts. [74] Thus: "*sì* preoccupato" (16), "*sì* tosto" (20), "*sì* leggermente" (32), "*sì* tardi" (44), "*sì* mirabilmente" (47), et al.; and "*così* poco" (371), "*così* giovane, *così* debole" (397), "*così* immacolatamente"

---

[73] See Fornaciari, *Sintassi,* p. 104; also Rohlfs, *Sintassi,* p. 304.
[74] See Fornaciari, *Sintassi,* p. 260.

(399), *"così* passeggiere" (E.81), *"così* strano, *così* indifferente" (E.134), et al.

2.7.12. The clear preference for *assai* over its synonyms *molto* and the more rarely applied *troppo* [75] is traceable to the Sicilian (or Southern) element. Although there are many exceptions, the general tendency with these adverbs of quantity is that while *assai* precedes mainly the adjectives ("*assai* bruno" -27, "*assai* distinta" -39, "*assai* comuni" -41, "*assai* grande" -55, "*assai* applaudito" -70, and so on), *molto* and *troppo* usually appear with verbs, other adverbs and adverbial clauses ("odiava *troppo* ancora" -51, "è sopravvenuto *troppo* improvvisamente" -119, "*troppo* in furia" -354, "*molto* spesso" -E.85, "*molto* caldo" -31, "*troppo* caldo" -412, "Ho *molto* sofferto" -358, "era *troppo* donna" -E.94, et al.).

2.7.13. An occasional favorite is also the literary *alquanto* as a quantitative adverb: "*alquanto* gravemente" (19), "lo calmarono *alquanto*" (45), "*alquanto* più di libertà" (47), "*alquanto* malinconici" (86), "ti calunnii *alquanto*" (377), "*alquanto* pensierosa" (E.21), "*alquanto* più alto di lei" (E.23), "*alquanto* fredda" (E.73), "parve riflettere *alquanto*" (E.137), "abbuiandosi *alquanto*" (E.156), et al.

2.8.1a. A great deal of inconstancy is shown in the handling of certain prepositions. It is not rare, for example, for *a*, sometimes followed by the article, to make a pleonastic appearance; this is especially true when it appears with the word *sera*, even where no particular happening is intended: [76] "Ieri *a* sera, ti rammenti?" (166), "siamo qui da ieri *a* sera" (180), "perchè fai così tardi *alla* sera?" (E.25), "ritornando *alla* sera" (E.58). As for other cases: "applaudivano *alle* sue parole" (62), "Ore che son ritornata presso *alla* mia buona Filomena" (187).

2.8.1b. The Sicilian influence makes itself felt in the cases where the sense of future is expressed by *avere* + *a* + *infin.*: [77]

---

[75] Rohlfs, *Sintassi*, p. 289, states that *molto* and *troppo* are virtually unknown south of Rome.

[76] Fornaciari, *Sintassi*, p. 335: "*A* segna con precisione il punto o il momento di tempo, in cui accade qualche cosa."

[77] *Ibid.*, p. 197; also Rohlfs, *Sintassi*, p. 84. See also T. Ebneter, "Aviri a + infinitif' et le probleme du futur en Sicilien," *Cahiers Ferdinand de Saussure*, 23 (1966), 39.

"per ascoltare quello che *aveva a dirmi*" (103), "quante cose *avrò a dirti*" (176), "*ho a farti* un discorso serio" (E.38). Today, in cases of the sort, the preposition *da* is more usual.

2.8.2a. A certain flexibility is shown at times in the choice between *a* and *in*. With the names of cities, for example, both prepositions are found: "*in* Napoli" (12, 64), "*in* Siracusa" (12), "*in* Firenze" (247); but also: "*a* Napoli" (64), et al. The phrase (*mettersi*) *in letto* is preferred to the more usual (*mettersi*) *a letto*: "stando *in letto* tutta sola" (175), "ero *in letto*" (350), "la indusse (…) a *mettersi in letto* vicino al suo bimbo" (392), "*si mise in letto* colla febbre" (401). *In* is also preferred to *a* in cases similar to the following: "la rividi *in* una festa" (86), "*in* una festa da ballo" (341), "che rividi qui *in* una certa cena" (E.101), "andai ad attenderla *in* casa sua" (272); with the names of months: "Io partirò *in* giugno" (247), "Io ci andrò forse *in* dicembre" (248), "Le signore Manfredini sarebbero andate *in* giugno a Livorno" (E.85), "Il matrimonio fu celebrato *in* ottobre" (E.151).

2.8.2b. In some instances the appearance of *in* is redundant: "Ciò che ho detto *in* quella sera" (E.80), "non ti do torto, no, *in* parola d'onore…" (E.140).

2.8.3a. The largest amount of oscillation appears with *di*. With verbs such as *tentare, cercare, credere, sperare, mostrare* and *rincrescere, di* is often missing before the infinitive: "come se avesse cercato interpretare" (75), "cercando illudermi spesso" (119), "tentando inumidire l'aridità" (126-27), "cercando trasfondere la vita" (127), "tentando strapparlo" (127), "cercava rassegnarsi" (131), "tentò rompere" (153), "cerco vincere me stessa" (154), "tento difendermi" (159), "tenta confortarmi" (186), "cerco dissimularlo" (203), "tentavano rubarla" (326), "che avea creduto conoscere" (337), "cercando dare un sapore" (340), "tentava trattenerla" (345), "speravo vedervi" (358), "tentai prendergli una mano" (380), "sperando rivedere" (E.27), "mostrava non aver perdonato" (E.79), "cerco rianimare colla briglia" (E.125), "avea tentato dissipar la tenue nube" (E.161). In many other instances, however, *di* is present: "cercando *di* dare" (45), "avrei temuto *di* carezzarla" (90), "teme *d'*incontrarsi in me" (120), "mi pare *di* fare un torto" (139), "mi rimproverò *di* averla spaventata" (142), "mi pareva *di* svenire" (162), "Evitò *d'*incontrarlo" (157), "mi pare *d'*impazzire" (171), "cercare *d'*indovinare" (181), "Non vorrei mai lasciare *di* chiacchierare con te" (196), "mi pare *di* essere pazza" (204), "credevo *di* sognare" (247), "mi pare *di* amarti davvero" (260), "non cercava *di* leggerle in cuore" (396), "godeva *di* vederla assisa" (411). The author is much more attentive in dealing with the verb *osare,* always followed by *di*: "non *osava* *d'*incontrare un viso ch'egli voleva vadere" (61), "non *osava di* farlo" (61), "senza *osare di* fiatare" (410), "senza *osare di* fissare" (E.33), "senza *osare di* guardarlo" (E.39), "senza *osare di* svelargli" (E.51), "non *oserebbe di* fare" (E.124).

2.8.3*b*. There are also instances where *di* can be considered pleonastic: "Non occorre *di* suggellarlo" (80), "avrei desiderato tanto *di* vederti" (180), "Non voglio *della* tua compassione" (235), "fissò su *di* Giorgio (...) uno sguardo limpido e ghiacciato" (325), "siamo fuori *di* pericolo" (391), "guardava *di* sottecchi" (E.29, E.154), "Dopo *di* avere attraversato due altre sale" (E.74), "andò a cercare *del* colonello Marteni" (E.136), "Tra *di* loro due che s'amavano tanto (...) c'era sempre un abisso" (E.155).

2.8.3*c*. Verga is always very careful in placing *di* after the preposition *verso* when the personal pronoun follows. The care, however, is unnecessarily applied even to cases where the name of a person is found in place of the pronoun. In addition to *verso di me* (278), *verso di lui* (32), *verso di noi* (373), et al. one also finds: "si avanzò (...) *verso di Brusio*" (56, 57), "voltavasi *verso di Alberto*" (E.19, E.127), et al. In the case of other substantives, other than personal nouns *di* does not appear: "levar la testa *verso* il coro" (205), "s'incamminò (...) *verso* la villa" (E.188), "si incamminò *verso* casa" (E.92).

2.8.4. *Da* used as a complement of quality is extremely common in these pages: "bel personaggio *da* dramma o *da* romanzo" (32), "riso *da* sirena" (43), "corpo *da* fata" (47, 83, 88), "mani *da* fata" (85, 91), "femmine *da* trivio" (59, 60), "positura *da* sirena" (84), "sorriso *da* sirena" (88), "maniere *da* educanda" (146), "aria *da* statua" (333), "abbraccio *da* lupa" (381), "esclamazioni *da* trivio"

(245), "fiore *da* stufa" (E.17), "*da* uomo onnipotente" (E.87), and so on.

2.8.5. To the Southern norm might be traced the decisive preference for *sino* over *fino* (although even the Florentine vernacular favors the former form):[78] "Scopriamo *sin* dal principio il meccanismo" (18), "a camminare *sin* fuori porta Garibaldi" (28), "*sino* a quattro per la toletta" (36), "correrò *sino* a Siracusa" (94), "suscitate *sino* al parossismo" (105), "debba salire *sino* a Lui" (138), "per andare *sino* a Trecastagne" (181), "*sino* all'ultimo momento" (233), "*sin* quasi a soffiargli in faccia le parole" (303), "*sino* ai trent'anni" (321), "l'accompagnò *sino* alla carrozza" (344), "vi occuperete di lui *sino* a' sette anni" (E.12), "si arrampica *sino* al tuo davanzale?" (E.25), "gentiluomo *sino* alla punta delle unghie" (E.122), et al. In contrast to these examples, there are few with *fino*: "vennero a trovarci *fin* dallo spuntare del giorno" (150), "odiando *fin* anche il pensiero di essere vicino" (52), "*fin* sull'immagine del marito (397).

2.9.1. Verga is very favorable to certain conjunctions containing the particle *che*. Among these, the temporal *allorchè* is by far the most predominant: "le amerò *allorchè* scoprirò un cuore nella donna" (24), "*allorchè* il sole è più cocente" (133), "*Allorchè* ringrazio il Signore (. . .) lo faccio con una parola" (134), "*Allorchè* riaprì gli occhi mi sembrò di vedere un cadavere" (233), "*allorchè* ricevetti il biglietto che m'invitava" (319), "come soleva fare nel passato *allorchè* desiderava vederlo" (351), "*Allorchè* questo dubbio fatale è entrato in me" (E.80), et al.

2.9.2. As opposed to *allorchè* the subordinate propositions introduced by *quando* are relatively few, but those introduced by *allorquando* are more numerous: "*Allorquando* i due amici si avvicinarono a lei, ella si era fermata dinanzi a un camino" (325), "*Allorquando* lo strascico superbo di Velleda frusciava sul tappeto vicino a lui" (E.41), "*allorquando* avea sentito il bisogno di aver fiducia nel sentimento che riempiva tutto il suo essere" (E.81), et al.

---

[78] See Rohlfs, *Sintassi,* p. 235. Rohlfs, however, tends to emphasize that *sino* is used primarily in the South.

2.9.3. Dacchè, finchè and *sinchè* also make an occasional appearance as temporal conjunctions: "*Dacchè* cotesta tentazione si è impossessata di me, io non mi riconosco più" (162), "*Dacchè* si era messo nella carriera diplomatica non ci eravamo visti che a rari intervalli" (319), "È stato sempre a Firenze (...) *dacchè* non ci siam visti?" (333), "ma *dacchè* ti son vicino ti amo" (E.35), "*sinchè* vi è tempo" (E.92), "Rimediamoci, *finchè* siamo in tempo" (E.92).

2.9.4. The Tuscan favored *poichè*[79] — rather than the more widely accepted *perchè* — is the conjunction mostly used to introduce a causal proposition: "*poichè* Raimondo ha la voce dolce ed insinuante" (17), "*poichè* non poteva giustificarla" (27), "*poichè* soltanto alcuni squarci attrassero la sua attenzione" (40), "*poichè* tutti tacevano" (145), "*poichè* suo figlio avrebbe dovuto lasciar l'omnibus alla solita fermata" (160), "*poichè* allentò le braccia" (270), "*poichè* starò qui due mesi" (369), "*poichè* a bucarsi la pelle c'è sempre tempo" (E.137), "*Poichè* ci siamo amati, non è così" (E.171), et al.

2.9.5. Quite popular in these works is also *giacchè*. Sometimes, just like *poichè*, it is used to introduce causal propositions: "Spero di farmi almeno un nome coi proverbi (...) *giacchè* non l'ho potuto con opere di maggior lena..." (21), "Tu vedi come ti amo, come son geloso, *giacchè* ti fo piangere" (277), "*giacchè* quel saluto gli avea tirato addosso l'attenzione generale" (302), "*giacchè* la fisonomia di lei avea ripreso subito la maschera rigida e calma" (345), "Li racconterò a te e a tuo marito, *giacchè* infine mi presenterai a tuo marito" (369). Most times, however, *giacchè* is found in the introductory part or in the premise of a syllogistic-like statement, whose conclusion, usually introduced by the correlatives *così* or *allora,* is often implied rather than stated. It is not unusual, therefore, to find *giacchè* with incomplete or elliptical sentences: "*Giacchè* siete tutti congiurati, e volete così..." (25), "*Giacchè* non ho il bene di conoscerne neanche il nome..." (34), "*Giacchè* il conte n'è uscito illeso, cosa deve importare di me (...) a quella signora?" (79), "*Giacchè* lo vuoi..." (97), "*Giacchè* non lo sa,

---

[79] *Ibid.,* p. 180.

o *giacchè* non si rammenta, tanto meglio ..." (336), "*Giacchè* non siamo ancora amici, *giacchè* non possiamo essere camerati, *giacchè* non saremo mai altro, siamo pure fratello e sorella" (339), "*giacchè* mi ragionate d'amore, ascoltate" (348), "È inutile che te lo dica, *giacchè* non mi conosci, e non mi conoscerai giammai" (E.71), "Ma *giacchè* li desidera ... glieli ha dati ..." (E.75), "*Giacchè* è scritto che le mie visite debbano giungere sempre in ritardo, vorrà permettermi di presentarmi a lei domani nella serata" (E.102), et al.

2.9.6. To denote a final aim or purpose, both *perchè* and *affinchè* are more or less equally applied: "raccomandami a Dio *perchè* io subisca codesta prova con rassegnazione" (185), "Vi lascerò procura *affinchè* possiate riscuotere da voi quella somma che crederete ..." (E.11).

2.9.7. Quite often the more literary *chè* [80] is found in place of the more conventional *perchè* in the causal constructions: "compiangimi, *chè* son molto triste" (152), "*chè* in Sicilia l'idea dell'ospedale stringe il cuore" (233), "ora andatevene, *chè* viene il conte" (299), "*chè* sentiva di essere ridicolo" (341), "*chè* lo vedevo a Firenze spendere a rotta di collo" (362), "*chè* noi dovevamo essere marito e moglie" (368), "*chè* così com'era situato il suo viso non si distingueva chiaramente" (375), "*chè* per tale ti ho? ..." (E.57), "*chè* non ci ho nessun merito" (E.94), "Ringraziatemene, cugina, *chè* me lo merito" (E.144), et al.

2.9.8a. The very predominant appearance of comparative and modal propositions introduced by *come* and, less often, by *quasi* has to be considered one of the characteristic traits of not only these novels but of the author's entire narrative. Of particular interest are the various and sometimes unusual ways in which these clauses are handled when they denote an hypothetical or conditional state. The particle *se,* for example, may or may not appear before the subjunctive. Thus: "*come se* avesse creduto (...) a quel sogno" (30), "*come se* temesse di destare un'eco" (83), "*come se* volesse farsi perdonare" (376), "*come se* aspettasse" (390), "*come se* vedesse" (E.20), "*come se* fosse un estraneo" (E.182), et al; and

---

[80] See Battaglia-Pernicone, p. 553.

"*come* avesse qualcosa che lo pungesse" (376), "*come* fosse in chiesa" (398), "*come* fosse un estraneo" (398), "*come* stessi per morire" (E.65), "*come* si accorgesse solo allora di lui" (E.72), et al.

2.9.8b. Frequently the literary *quasi* is found in place of the expected *come*: "*quasi* mi sembrasse poterle diradare col mio desiderio" (161), "*quasi* vedessero sorgersi dinanzi un fantasma" (394), "*quasi* non bastasse" (401), "*quasi* si sentisse morire" (403), "*quasi* volesse nascondervelo" (413), "*quasi* temesse di annoiarlo" (E.53), "*quasi* gli appartenessero" (E.109), et al.

2.9.8c. Very often the subjunctive that should follow *come* is replaced by the gerund, and this is one of the most unusual syntactical constructions in these pages: "diss'egli, *come rispondendo* a se stesso" (15), "rispose (...) Pietro, *come destandosi* di soprassalto" (18), "Poscia, *come arrossendo* del suo trasporto, si mise a ridere fragorosamente" (24), "quegli occhi dalla pupilla trasparente dovevavo fissarsi sui suoi, sebbene *come non vedendolo*" (27), "domandò egli *come parlando* in sogno" (44), "vi stava ad occhi chiusi, *come dormendo* ed assorbendo con maggior squisitezza di voluttà le armonie della musica" (48), "la contessa si fermò, anelante, *come cullandosi* al braccio del suo splendido cavaliere" (68), "domandai poscia, *come non accorgendomene*" (114), "e soggiunse *come parlando* a se stessa" (250), "ella mi disse, *come risovvenendosi*" (271), "La contessa si guardava attorno, *come cercando* un pretesto per rompere quel silenzio" (E.105), "domandò Alberti *come rispondendo* ad una lunga meditazione" (E.145), "Discorrevano a sbalzi (...) *come rispondendo* ai pensieri che andavano svolgendosi per la loro singolare situazione" (E.146), "Alberti levò il capo *come svegliandosi* (E.187), et al.

2.9.8d. Not unusual in these hypothetical comparative clauses is the presence of *come* followed by the infinitive, by *per* + *infinitive* and, on one or two occasions, by *a* + *infinitive*: "Pietro si sentì *come allargare* il cuore e fu grato all'amico" (26), "quella folla urlante che levava braccia nere (...) *come ad imprecare*, verso i palchetti" (62), "Ella si era stretta contro la parete (...) *come per farsene* schermo" (63), "Singhiozzante gli gettai le braccia al collo, *come per non lasciarmelo* sfuggire mai più" (96-97), "*come per scacciare* la penosa preoccupazione che ci aveva invaso" (100), "*come per ringraziarlo* e non lasciarlo" (128), "*come per vedere* con chi avesse da fare" (305), "*come per mettere* a sesto le sue idee" (E.97), "di tanto in tanto fermavasi *come per stare* in ascolto" (E.125).

2.9.8e. Another structure often adopted for the hypothetical construction is *come* followed by the adjective or the substantivized past participle: "indi, *come stanca* di quello sforzo" (31), "Indi, *come infastidita* da quello sguardo" (39), "*come sorpreso* che un giovane il quale indossava abiti piuttosto eleganti venisse a cercare una tal festa" (55), "*come sorpresa* di quella molesta assiduità" (40), "urtando contro i mobili *come ebbra...*" (120), "Pietro l'abbracciò (...) *come ebbro...* (121), "Apro gli occhi *come trasognata*" (193), "poscia, *come pentitosi*, rifacendosi scuro in volto" (237), "*come vergognosa* per quello che doveva dirmi" (270), "stette un momento a guardarlo, *come smemorata*" (389), "vedendolo rimase *come sbalordita*" (391), "Adele rimase *come fulminata*" (E.148), "pallida, *come trasognata*, gli rivolse un'occhiata paurosa" (E.150), et al. All these examples clearly show that in the subordinate clauses Verga is very much favorable to the implicit (infinite) forms.

2.10.1. The interjections appearing in these novels range from monosyllabic sounds to elliptical phrases and from conventional and literary forms to more immediate vocal expressions deriving from everyday speech.

While the expression *oh* is found primarily in *Eros* (pp. 16, 101, 118, 161, et al.), *ahimè* predominates in *Eva* (241, 243, 271, 279, 286, 288, 308, etc.).

To show surprise, both *per bacco* (and *perbacco*) and *to'*are favored: "*Per bacco!* ti credeva sui digesti" (29), "*Per bacco!* al ritratto che ne fai..." (37), "*Per bacco!* dopo aver veduto Narcisa agitata" (79), "è una donna pericolosa, *per bacco!*" (355), "*Perbacco!* esclamò con sinistro entusiasmo" (235), "*To...to...to!* Pietro, amico mio, ne saresti innamorato?..." (23), "*To'*, guarda!" (320), "*To'*! par vero? Eppure è proprio La Ferlita col suo marmocchio" (360), "*To'*! perchè ella mi ama" (E.32), "*To!* eri tu, biondino?" (E.119).

2.10.2. To the popular-like language belong the various exclamations containing the word *Dio*. This word appears in instances ranging from supplication to euphemistically intentioned outbursts: "Che donna...*Perdio*!..." (21), "*Perdio*!...E tu l'ami, costei?!..." (37), "*Perdio*! disse una voce secca ed orgogliosa" (50), "Siamo uomini, *perdio*!..." (53), "*Perdio*!...com'è bella!..." (244), "*Perdio*! (...). Non vien certamente la voglia di tornare a casa" (281), "*Perdio, s'è freddo!*" (281), "Oh, *mio Dio*!...ma ne ridi in un certo modo!..." (265), "*mio Dio*! che vita!!..." (88), "Qual vita ho fatta!...*Dio*! *Dio mio*!..." (94), "*Pel nome di Dio!*" (299), "*Dio sia benedetto!*" (174). Expressions with *diavolo!* (302), *Cristo!* (56), *diamine!* (E.38) are also present.

2.10.3. Also present are some expressions that cast light on the Sicilian sense of honor and pride, thus bringing to mind the forms that will be more common in works such as "Cavalleria rusticana," for example, and "La Lupa.": "*In fede mia* che ne ho abbastanza di tali amori da quindici anni!!..." (19), "*In fede mia!* (...) non avevo ancora pensato all'ospedale e al camposanto..." (236), "*Parola d'onore!* (...) che tu ne sei innamorato cotto" (19), "io l'ucciderò *com'è vero che mi chiamo Pietro Brusio* e che quest'uomo mi ha insultato a Catania..." (72-73), "*In parola d'onore* (...) voglio mettere tanto di catenaccio alla porta di casa!" (361).

2.10.4. The very frequent appearance of *o* before a question can also be registered within the list of interjections. With the exception of a couple of cases, this form is present only in *Eros* and there is no doubt that it reflects a closer adherence to the spoken Florentine:[81] "*O* dunque?" (242), "*O* perchè diventi rossa?" (370), "*O* come si fa allora?" (E.16), "*O* che non si va in giardino?" (E.18), "*O* cosa vuoi che venga a farci io?" (E.19), "*O* perchè?" (E.21), "*O* che fa lei costà, così mattiniera?" (E.23), "*O* cos'hai?" (E.28), "*O* tu perchè non sei venuto?" (E.51), "*O* come va che trovasi qui e solo?" (E.75), "*O* come va dunque che pensassi in quel momento ad un altro (...) ch'era anche un gran cattivaccio?" (E.175).

---

[81] See Rohlfs, *Sintassi*, pp. 157-159.

2.11.1. Although the most prevalent form of enunciation is the direct discourse — even the epistolary narrative can be regarded as an extended form of direct discourse — also present, but to a much lesser extent, is the indirect discourse. The change from the former to latter form is handled through the conventional means. The enunciation is usually preceded by a preposition or conjunction (*che, se, di*), and as for the tenses, the present is replaced by either the infinitive or imperfect, the past indicative by the pluperfect, the imperative by the subjunctive and the future by the conditional:[82]

> Al garzone che gli domandava cosa ordinasse, rispose di non saperlo, di recare quel che voleva (...) purchè l'accompagnasse di una bottiglia di marsala. (54)

> Pietro passò innanzi e mi porse la mano raccomandandomi di non guardare il precipizio per non avere la vertigine. (113)

> Mi accadde due o tre volte di non trovarla in casa, e non le domandai dove fosse stata. (285)

> Mi domandò se fossi in collera con lei, se avessi pensato a lei, se l'amassi ancora; mi disse che non mi aveva mai dimenticato, che era contenta di vedermi in quello stato, che era orgogliosa di avermi amato. (295)

> Giorgio senza finire quel che stava dicendo balbettò che andava a far delle visite, ed uscì. (373)

> La signora Ruscaglia cominciò a dire che quello spettacolo le faceva male .... (389)

> Verso mezzanotte Rendona (...) disse che andava a riposare un poco. (407)

2.11.2. Somewhat unique is one example of indirect discourse in *Storia di una capinera*: "Mia matrigna fece una scena; mi rimproverò che io *sono* una ragazza male educata, capricciosa, che mi abbandono a degli impeti di gioia e a degli accessi di malin-

---

[82] See Fornaciari, *Sintassi*, p. 414. Cf. N. Vita, "Genesi del 'discorso rivissuto' e suo uso nella narrativa italiana," *Cultura neolatina*, XV (1955), 5-6.

conia ingiustificabili" (159). The uniqueness of this example lies in the present form *sono* which, as one would expect, should have become *ero*. In this case the present is a subjective element indicating that the speaker is, at least in her altered state of mind, in agreement with the accusations that she is charged with. [83]

2.11.3. The subjective and the psychological element, however, is more characteristic of the *erlebte Rede*, a term accepted and used by scholars such as Lorck, Lerch and Spitzer and rendered into English, by Jespersen, as "experienced" or "represented" speech. [84] Even if these works contain relatively few examples of this predominantly stylistic device, it is important that they be pointed out since this expedient will be mastered and extensively applied by the author in his mature works, especially in *I Malavoglia*.

2.11.4. Perhaps aware of the fact that he was dealing with a still rather uncommon device and also because of his quite apparent wish of accentuating on the "impressionistic" [85] aspect of the spoken words, Verga will often present examples of *erlebte Rede* in italics. [86] These examples are generally of an imitative or mimical nature, thus coming closer to the spoken type of discourse. This group includes quotations from known works, nicknames, titles and single words of particular significance to the speaker and they are presented in fragmentary or, as Herczeg prefers, in "elliptical" [87] phrases that are often expressed with a touch of irony, be it the author's, the speaker's or that of a choral group. These examples are present from the very first novel:

---

[83] On the roles of the present in the indirect discourse, see E. Cane, *Il discorso indiretto libero* (Roma, 1969), esp. pp. 100-101.

[84] O. Jespersen, *The Philosophy of Grammar* (New York, 1924), pp. 290-91.

[85] L. Spitzer, "L'originalità della narrazione nei *Malavoglia*," *Belfagor*, XI (1956), 47: "L'*erlebte Rede* rende 'impressionisticamente' quello che poteva udire il narratore."

[86] It should be pointed out that in addition to indicating foreign words or expressions, the italicized print is freely used by the author whenever he wishes to accentuate the emotive power that certain words might have for the speaker. A good example of this would be the many italicized personal pronouns (*lui, lei, ella*, etc.) found in all novels and especially in *Storia di una capinera*.

[87] G. Herczeg, *Lo stile indiretto libero in italiano* (Firenze, 1963), p. 16.

In seguito amai una fanciulla . . . *pura siccome un angiolo,* come direbbe il signor Germont nella *Traviata.* (20)

Brusio non era più uno straniero per loro, un *signorino,* ora che maneggiava sì bene il bastone. (57)

ella mi fece chiamare *misteriosamente . . . segretamente,* capisce? (79)

Non c'era che dire, quei due bravi giovanotti si scannavano *da perfetti gentiluomini.* (306)

Il *dottore dal cappello bianco* s'inginocchiò presso del conte (...) e gli aprì la camicia. (307)

La credo una leggiadra bionda — non bella ma leggiadra — molto elegante, che *fa bene* in un salone . . . . (330)

e arrivando all'improvviso seppi che durante la mia lontananza egli aveva avuto *una distrazione* . . . . (350)

A sedici anni Alberto era un giovanetto alto e delicato (. . .) — *un ingegno che vi sgusciava dalle mani ad ogni istante* — diceva il suo professore di filosofia. (E.13)

Uno dei vicini aveva recato una gran notizia : si aspettava *la contessa* in villa Armandi — la bella contessa Emilia — dicevasi. (E.29)

le propose sul serio *una capanna e il suo cuore* (E.139).

Se non si fosse trattato che di lui, ella avrebbe continuato ad essere la migliore amica di Adele, e del resto — a parte il principe, che nell'esistenza di Velleda non avea giammai contato altro che come principe — l'antico suo amante era davvero divenuto un *cencio d'uomo.* (E.165)

Al concerto c'era tutto il *mondo elegante,* all'infuori della principessa Metelliani. (E.169)

The reader will notice that, occasionally, Verga's still uncertain handling of this device can be detected by his insertion of *dire,* a verb that becomes unnecessary — and therefore redundant — whenever this form is correctly applied.

2.11.5.   There are other examples, however, where the so called "experienced speech," through the enunciative and narrative modes,[88] manifests itself in a more fluent and spontaneous manner and its application, rather than carrying ironic innuendos, serves primarily to mingle the spoken word with the narration:

> Si raccontavano dicendo le loro conquiste, le loro civetterie e le loro follie di giovinezza; tempo addietro, gli raccontava, si era invaghita di un giovane studente, proprio quel che si dice un gran monello, ma bello, bello da dipingere, con occhi neri grandi così, e un collo fatto come quello dell'Antinoo, un collo che bisognava vedere allorquando snodava la sua cravatta rossa e sbottonava il colletto della camicia per giocare alla palla fuori porta San Gallo. (340-41)

> Lo zio (...) rispose ringraziando, come meglio sapeva e poteva, il signor direttore per l'ottima riuscita del giovanetto — una lettera che fece montare la mosca al buon direttore — come se lo si volesse minchionare, e non era vero! (E.14-15)

> Lo zio Bartolomeo, da uomo che sa fare le cose, avea preparato al nipote una grata sorpresa. (E.28)

> Però fu tormentato tutta la notte dal dubbio, combinato colla tosse dello zio, che quella tal persiana non fosse stata sempre socchiusa, come l'avea vista rientrando — e di vento non ne avea tirato una maledetta in tutta la sera. (E.37)

> Dopo un par d'ore (...) venne a sapere che lo zio Bartolomeo (...) le rimanenti lire 3876,97 le consegnava al momento. Ben inteso senza voler sentire nemmeno discorrere d'indennità — diamine! non era del medesimo sangue per nulla! Alberto gli rammentava al viso la sua povera Cecilia! (E.38)

> Sovente sorprendeva gli occhi di lei che lo fissavano carichi di collera, accigliati, foschi; allora il riso di lei era più mordente, o, cosa strana, la sua parola era più graziosa. (E.77)

> Le signore chiudevano un occhio sulle stranezze di lui perchè egli li aveva molto belli tutti e due, era giovane e ricco, e qualche volta anche grazioso ed amabile. (E.115)

---

[88] For further explanation of the "enunciative" and "narrative" types of *erlebte Rede*, see N. Vita, pp. 5-6.

The fact that most examples, as the illustrations above show, appear in *Eros*[89] is most significant for it further demonstrates that the author's intentions of heading toward the new "veristic" horizons were already present at this time.[90]

2.12.1. One final aspect that cannot be overlooked, since it is a characterizing factor of this prose, is the prolific repetition of identical forms and groups of words in successive clauses. On the syntactical level this device helps in establishing the author's decisive preference for the paratactical structures and, on the stylistic level, it accentuates the dramatic impact that he wishes to convey. These anaphoric forms, very reminiscent of D'Annunzio's oratorical prose, contribute in setting, to use Gutia's words, "un ritmo incalzante" that serves to "accrescere il volume e l'intensità dello stato d'animo"[91] of the characters and the narrator. The success achieved by the author is at times somewhat debatable. Here are some examples taken at random: "si avanzò sul parapetto (...) *colle* braccia (...) *col* suo sorriso sulle labbra (...) *con* quel piccolo grappolo d'uva" (61), "*colle mie* debolezze, *coi miei* errori, *colla mia* colpa, *coll'*immensurabile amore che vi porto" (210), "*con una* parola graziosa, *con un* sorriso, *con un'*occhiata" (E.89), "apparve una scena incantata, riboccante *di* suoni, *di* luce, *di* veli, e *di* larve seducenti che turbinavano (...) come una fantasgamoria *di* sorrisi affascinanti, *di* forme leggiadre, *di* occhi lucenti e *di* capelli sciolti" (240), "pieno *di* vita, *di* cuore, *di* memorie e *d'*immaginazione" (292), "un non so che *di* attonito, *d'*ansioso, *d'*irato, *di* vendicativo, *d'*innamorato e *di* pauroso" (E.115), "corruscante febbrili desideri *dal* sorriso impudico, *dagli* occhi arditi, *dai* veli che gettavano ombre irritanti (...) *dai* procaci pudori, *dagli* omeri sparsi di biondi capelli, *dai* brillanti falsi, *dalle* pagliuzze dorate, *dai* fiori artificiali" (240), "*dalle* folte e morbide chiome cinerine, *dai* grand'occhi azzurri e dalle labbra rugiadose" (E.17), "*nel* mutato contegno dello sposo, *nelle* sue attenzioni impacciate e timide, *nelle* sue distrazioni, *nelle*

---

[89] We cannot agree, therefore, with Vita, who says, on p. 24, that *Eros* has no examples of *erlebte Rede*.

[90] Vita, p. 14, states that the *erlebte Rede* satisfies the exigencies of "verismo" and is therefore very popular at this time.

[91] "Sull'uso della preposizione 'con' nella prosa italiana contemporanea," *L. N.*, XIV (1953), 16.

sue preoccupazioni frequenti" (394), "*nella* parola, *nell*'accento, *nella* fisonomia e *nell*'atteggiamento" (E.114), "Egli suggeva avidamente coi baci *per la* fronte, *pei* capelli, *per le* labbra, *per gli* occhi, *pel* collo quelle emanazioni acri" (121), "era ritornata a Firenze (. . .) e *per* consiglio dei medici, *per* obbligo di condizione, *per* svago, *per* far piacere alla figliuola" (E.161), "io corsi a rinchiudermi nel mio camerino, *a* piangere, *a* ridere, *a* singhiozzare liberamente, *ad* abbracciare i piedi del crocifisso, i mobili, le pareti" (162), "Vi amo *perchè* siete ingenuo, *perchè* non siete ricco, *perchè* non siete elegante, *perchè* avete il cuore in tutte le follie dell'arte, *perchè* mi guardate con quegli occhi" (257), "T'amo *perchè* mi ami così, *perchè sei* matto, *perchè sei* geloso, *perchè sei* ingiusto e cattivo" (274), "mi domandò dei miei amori, *e* come amassi, *e* come fossi amato, *e se* amassi di più o in un altro modo, — *e* mi diede anche un bacio come mi avrebbe dato una stretta di mano" (296), "quell'uomo, quel soldato, *sì* giovane, *sì* bello, *sì* splendido! che le parlava *sì* da presso" (71), "*questa donna* che ha il sorriso ammaliatore (. . .), *questa donna* mi ama! (. . .). *Questa donna* io l'ho posseduta (. . .). Raimondo, sai tu cos'è *questa donna*? (. . .). *Questa donna* che vivea dei piaceri (. . .) *questa donna* non esce più quasi mai" (90-91), "Sì, *io son* vile! *io son* colpevole! *io sono* infame!" (117), "*della quale* i tratti (. . .); *della quale* gli occhi si dilatavano (. . .); *della quale* infine le labbra si aprivano" (123), "*Vorrei* strapparmi i capelli; *vorrei* lacerarmi il petto colle unghie; *vorrei* urlare come una belva" (204), "Pensai ad Eva *che non* era ricca, *che non* era gran dama, *che non* aveva un bel nome, a *che* era nella condizione di dover smungere la borsa dei suoi amanti" (292), "Ora (. . .) provava *lo stesso* sentimento d'inquietudine, *lo stesso* sbigottimento, *lo stesso* bisogno di attaccarsi a qualche cosa" (395), "Alberti la vedeva *in tutte* le riunioni, *in tutte* le partite di campagna, e *in tutte* le traversate sul lago" (E.116).

LEXICON

3.0.1. The vocabulary of a literary work is always the product of two interrelated linguistic factors: the conventional norm or norms from which the expressive material is extracted and the very personal process of how such material is treated by the author. [1] This chapter, in addition to focusing attention on the degree of influence exerted by the various norms (i.e. Tuscan and Florentine, literary and Sicilian), will examine the terms and expressions which, by way of their arrangement and organization in a determined hierarchy, present themselves as "mots-temoins" and "mots-clés," as Matorè calls them, [2] and will also consider the themes, images and general artistic devices that tend to distinguish Verga's style on the lexical level.

3.1.1. It can be safely stated that while Verga's technical and linguistic skills do not often correspond to his "calore giovanile dell'ispirazione," [3] — and this is especially true at the beginning of this period — he does give, like any good artist, indications that his expressive elements are primarily directed at delineating the psychology, and in few instances the poetry, of the characters and of the general situation. Verga is keenly aware of the expressive ingredients that he has to deal with in order to present the society and the characters that interest him. He conforms to the high and fashionable society with all its "femmes fatales," sophistication and cosmopolitanism by adopting specific idiolects that reflect its cul-

---

[1] Cf. C. Schick, *Il linguaggio,* 3rd ed., PBE (Torino, 1964), p. 200.

[2] *La methode de lexicologie. Domaine française* (Paris, 1953), p. 65. For further explanation of these terms see also S. Ullman, *The Principles of Semantics,* 2nd ed. (New York, 1957), pp. 312-13.

[3] B. Croce, *La letteratura della nuova Italia* (Bari, 1949), III, 9.

tural interests, tastes and habits as well as its mannerisms and affectations.

3.1.2. The extensive selection of lexemes allotted to women and especially to the "femmes fatales" echoes a significant aspect of this beau monde's mannerisms. These forms — many of them of a rather exotic nature — easily lend themselves to a hierarchical semantic system when seen within a context and appraised through the various functional elements or "semes,"[4] embodied in them.

3.1.2a. *Femmina,* the few times that it appears, is used always in a pejorative and morally negative sense: "*femmine* di mala vita" (54), "fu (. . .) col massimo piacere degli spettatori, comprese le *femmine,* che questi assistettero a quel duello" (57), "egli, che aveva avuto ribrezzo a toccare la mano di quella *femmina,* spudorata corifea della festa" (59), "*femmine* da trivio" (59, 60).

3.1.2b. Of a more denotative nature are the terms *dama,* prevalent mostly in the first novel, *signora* and the much more frequent *donna.* All three are attributed to the description of well-to-do, fashionable and often beautiful women of an established higher social level: "Domani andrò ai Fiorentini — disse la *dama*" (65), "la *dama* domandò" (82), "Pietro si avanzò (. . .) verso la *dama*" (84), "le più eleganti e belle *dame*" (101), "Se quelle *dame* si fossero data la pena" (361), "erasi incaponito (. . .) della *dama*" (E.116), et al.; "chi vuol fare la corte ad una *signora*" (33), "*signora* di mezza età" (65), "la bella *signora*" (82), "leggiadra *signora*" (336), "coteste gran *signore* tisiche che vengono dal Nord" (364), "la *signora* più vicina non volse nemmeno il capo" (E.82), "L'argomento comincia ad annoiare coteste *signore*" (E.96), et al.; "La bella *donna*!" (15), "passarono quasi rasente a quella *donna*" (22), "si mette allo specchio *donna* per sortirne silfide" (23), "questa *donna*! questa *donna*! . . ." (63, also 90, 91), "parlando alla *donna* matura" (65), "belle *donne*" (239, 364, E.158), "Se sapeste che cos'è per una *donna* il

---

[4] Cf. A. J. Greimas, *Sémantique structurale* (Paris, 1966). See pp. 30-54 especially. In brief, Greimas defines "sèmes" as semantic distinctive traits that define and determine a term-object or lexeme. For a fuller and more detailed study on the meaning and relative function of "sèmes," see pp. 5-54 in this same book.

sapere di aver tanto piaciuto!" (257), "*donne* leggiadre" (E.44, E.152), et al.

3.1.2c. No ironic allusion is hinted at by *matrona,* a form that appears only in *Tigre reale* and used only in reference to model married women and mothers that act with discretion and sedateness: "le intime amiche e le *matrone* facevano corona alla moglie di Giorgio" (360), "Le *matrone* intime della famiglia se n'erano andate lasciando le ultime raccomandazioni" (365), "adesso sei una *matrona,* hai dei figli!" (368).

3.1.2d. On one occasion *donnina* is used to indicate an endearing and affectionate housewife. When Eva goes to live with Enrico, he says: "mi pareva che la fata fosse svanita, e non rimanesse più che una bella *donnina* — di quelle che piacciono — ma io avevo bisogno di adorarla!" (279). *Donniciuola,* on the other hand, is used both in a pejorative sense and in the description of a poor, unfortunate human being. An example of the first case is seen in *Eva,* when Enrico goes backstage and expresses his disappointment in seeing Eva at close range: "cotesta dea (...) si allaccia le scarpe come l'ultima *donnicciuola*" (244). An example of the second case is found in *Capinera,* where Maria sees herself as "una povera *donniciuola* infermiccia ed uggiosa" (191).

3.1.2e. Because of their more unusual nature, other forms become much more conspicuous. Aside from the fact that all these forms take the beauty of these women for granted, they also possess other distinctive connotative shades. *Vergine* is used to designate a young, pure, serene and innocent woman: "La giovanetta lo fissò collo sguardo limpido e franco della *vergine*" (E.36), "negli occhi sereni e nell'ingenuo sorriso della *vergine*" (E.36), "il limpido sguardo della *vergine*" (E.48); *angelo* and *angioletto* imply primarily unaffected loveliness, sweetness and, at times, also innocence: "Tu sei un *angelo* di bellezza, ed io ne sono orgoglioso di te" (97), "Venti ancor più belle di lei non farebbero un *angioletto* così bello e perfetto qual è la *piccina*" (23), "mio dolce *angioletto*" (88), "Com'è bella! non è vero? — Sì, è un *angioletto*" (E.32). *Dea* is synonymous with the striking beauty, charm, dignity and, occasionally, distance that these women exhibit: "faceva discernere le *dea* dal suo cocchio superbo" (227), "C'è il dispetto di aver visto il mio cuore ginocchioni dinanzi a cotesta *dea*" (244), "la *dea* si stancò per la prima" (294), "la *dea* mi largiva parole e sorrisi" (294), "La *dea* aveva un altro genere di sguardi" (295), "e la tua *dea*? (. . .). Quella del Pagliano, la superbiosa" (296). While *regina* is at times used to characterize the majestic countenance of these goddesses ("si fece largo davanti a quella *regina* che passava" -229, "stava come una *regina*" -E.47), their movements are often compared to those of a *silfide,* when graceful and delicate (e.g. 23; also "Narcisa ballò come una *silfide*" -66, "quel corpo leggiero da *silfide*" -68, "era la *silfide* dietro la scena" -243), and to those of a *sultana* when languid and lethargic ("si vedeva una figura di donna [. . .] con tutto il languente e voluttuoso abbandono di una *sultana*" -31, "gli gittò come una *sultana* il suo fazzoletto ricamato" -E.47).

Their passionate desires and feelings are, at times, equated to those of a *leonessa*: "Si diceva avesse spinto al suicidio il solo uomo che avesse mai amato (. . .), un amore da *leonessa*" (324), "le avea dato le febbri da *leonessa*" (327), "Nata si voltò come una *leonessa* ferita" (345).

3.1.2f. Also present are various terms that cast light on the bewitching and eventually destructive powers of these women. Their graceful appearance and excessive beauty are often described with the help of *fata* ("quella *fata,* che aveva fatto il fascino di tutti" -10, "corpo da *fata*" - 47, 83, 88, "mani da *fata*" - 85, 91, "La *fata* si curvò mollemente verso di lui" -87). But when their beauty contributes to the moral downfall of the men that have so foolishly become infatuated with them, they are pictured as vain and untrue *larve* ("*larve* seducenti" -240, "per correre dietro a *larve* affascinanti" —254, "faceva correre il mio pensiero stanco dietro certe *larve* senza forme precise" -289) and as deceptive *maghe, sirene* and *maliarde* ("si mette allo specchio donna per sortirne [. . .] *maga* ... *sirena* ... " -23, "Ella gli sorrideva del suo sorriso da *sirena*" -43, 88, "Narcisa, la *sirena* che gli avrebbe fatto adorare l'inferno" -76, "nella sua positura da *sirena*" -84, "cotesta *sirena* che abbaglia la ragione" -244, "Perchè sei venuta dunque, *maliarda*?" -297, "*Sirena! maliarda!* che mi aveva inebbriato co l'amore" - 298).

3.1.3. The list of lexemes assigned to the men is not as rich but, in addition to the conventional *uomo,* there are some forms used primarily in a derisive and at times also in a pejorative sense. The *Tigre reale,* Giorgio La Ferlita is caricatured once as a *farfallino* (321) because of his instability and fickleness but the author is more mordant in describing some of the stereotyped characters of this society: "seguitò colui, assumendo (. . .) l'aria misteriosa gonfia del vecchio *ganimede* che si crede sicuro del fatto suo" (78), "egli era sempre preferito a tutti quei *ganimedi* che gli davano uggia" (E.166), "Si vedeva anche qualche *donnino* elegante quasi smarrito in mezzo alla folla" (230), "i *numi dell'olimpo fiorentino* si pigiavano come ad una mostra" (294), "Sua moglie era sempre assediata da una folla di *cortigiani*" (E.158), "Il principe Don Ferdinando Metelliani era un *omiciattolo* dieci o dodici volte milionario" (E.86).

3.1.4. The rather prominent presence of diminutives ending in *-ino* is also a definite reflection of this society's conventional expression but it also casts light on one of the specific preferences of the Florentine milieu. Massimiliano Cardini points out in his study that the *-ino* ending is very popular with "il buon popolo fiorentino" but that its exaggerated use is at times ridiculed by Italians of other regions. [5] Verga's treatment of these forms seems to follow a somewhat analogous line. While he uses them to imitate the speech patterns of this social group the reader will also sense, especially toward the end of these novels (when the author has become disenchanted with this society), a shade of irony in the presence of these forms. It may be due partly to this reason, in fact, that these forms will tend to become more outstanding in the later phase of this period.

3.1.4a. These diminutives are widely used for the delineation of female characters. Almost all these "femmes fatales" are endowed with a *testolina* (91, et al.) (or *piccola testa* -68) "bionda" (228, 269), "leggiadra" (32, 261, E.33), "ricciuta" (122), "ornata" (39) and "coronata di fiori" (48), (while the men of this society are once described as having "*testine* così ben pettinate" -239). In addition

---

[5] Cf. "L'*ino* del parlar fiorentino," *L. N.,* V (1943), 35.

to this, Eva, for example, is presented with a "*corpicino* delicato" (250), a "leggiadra *figurina*" (255) and as having "*manine* tremanti" (255) and *piedini* (250, 295) with *stivalini* (296). And when she tells Enrico what she would do if she were not a ballerina: "Sai tu che cosa sarei senza la mia *gonnellina* corta e le mie *scarpine* di raso? Sarei (...) una ragazza che potrebbe dirsi *bellina* se non avesse gli *stivalini* rotti e il *cappellino* di traverso ..." (267). In *Tigre reale*, Giorgio, who is un "*tantino* materialista" (321), spends good part of his time with Nata, a *fanciullina* (321) who lives in a *villino* (331, 337). In *Eros*, Velleda is also known as "la *contessina* Manfredini" (15), Alberto as "*marchesino* Alberti" (13) and Adele, affectionately known as *Adelina* (21), in addition to having a "pura *figurina*" (49) and "candide *manine*" (49), is described as being *magrina* (17) with a *cuoricino* (52) that is a "tesoro."

3.1.4b. Other diminutives that are based on the Florentine norm and that clearly denote a social affectation are found in the following phrases: "siccome la notte era *freddina* si strinse al mio braccio" (250), "il discorso si metteva sul *freddino*" (319), "facendo ammirare a coloro che lo volevano (...) una *cosina* informe" (360), "quelle dame (...) ne avrebbero sentite delle *belline*" (361), "Quella fontana lì ce l'ho voluta io (...) non è *bellina*? *Bellina* tanto!" (E.20), "Ti piace codesto fiore? ... *Bellino*! come si chiama?" (E.24).

3.1.5. The frequency of diminutives — as well as other altered forms (see sec. 2.3.3) — appearing in *Storia di una capinera* fulfills, however, a somewhat different function. Rather than echoing the norm of a particular society, here the diminutives reflect primarily Maria's hyperbolical way of seeing. At the beginning of the story she is really a twenty-year-old sensitive child who, in her happiness at being temporarily free in the country, expresses her idyllic sentiments through endearing terms: *uccelletti* (131, 133, 136, 139, 140, 143, 149, 172, et al.), *fiorellini* (133, 139, 152, 196, 201, 210), *monticelli* (134), *altarino* (134), *giardinetto* (201), *casetta* (135, 136, 142, 145, 149, 173, 176, et al), *cameretta* (136, 157, 168, 173), *camerino* (140, 147, 162, 175), *capannuccia* (136, 174, 179, 180, 181, 182, 185), *famigliuola* (136, 149, 175), *stanzino* (136, 159, 172, 176, 179), *mazzolino* (150), *lettuccio* (140, 172, 180), *fogliuzze* (143, 200), *finestrella* (157), *farfalletta* (196, 201, 210). By the same token, a pejorative ending is added to terms that carry, in the text, a negative connotation: *peccataccio* (141, 147, 149, 157), *gattaccio* ("un brutto *gattaccio* mi fece provare un grande spavento" -141, "quel *gattaccio* nero, che allungava lo zampino per adunghiarlo" -142, "Io l'odio quel *gattaccio*" -142). It is important to note that in this novel, since the author's intention for using these terms is different, many of the diminutives do not end in -*ino*.

3.1.6. Certain adjectives, nouns and elative forms (see sec. 2.3.3) also contribute to the affective nature of this society. Before looking at them it should be stated that as Verga progresses with his work, his language will become more rigid and as a result a much tighter control will be practiced in the application of these terms. It appears, therefore, that at the beginning of this period the verbosity that exists, [6] which, as Cecchetti has noted, sometimes approaches an "indice di banalità," [7] is due, at least in part, to Verga's reaction, conscious or subconscious as it may have been, to his own still limited expressive abilities.

A very important role is played by many of the attributives ending in -*ante* and -*ente*: *affascinante* (68, 121, 227, 240), *anelante* (243), *ardente* (27, 53, 87, 91, 98, 102, 106, 114, 118, 326, 338, 373, et al.), *delirante* (70, 89, 93, 98, 152), *desolante* (262), *divorante* (59, 87, 110, 118, 121, 263, E.128), *febbricitante* (241, E.66, et al.), *fervente* (95, 101), *inebbriante* (44, 47, 84, 85, 90, 116, 121, et al.), *lacerante* (105), *palpitante* (227, 263), *penetrante* (333, E.99), *rovente* (51), *scintillante* (323, 327, 345), *seducente* (87, et al.), *sfrenante* (114), *straziante* (53, 109, 127), *tremante* (99), *trepidante* (97), *tripudiante* (E.72) and others. These forms — most of them of exotic nature (for further examples see sec. 2.3.1) — in addition to reflecting the influence received by the author from the so called "sfocati" [8] writers of the late Italian Romantic period, because of their high resonance, harmonize with the intensely passionate mood

---

[6] Due partly to this reason, Verga himself repudiated *Una peccatrice*, on the occasion of this work's reprint in 1892. Cf. introductory note to 1965 Mondadori edition.

[7] *Leopardi e Verga* (Firenze, 1962), p. 121.

[8] U. Bosco, "Preromanticismo e Romanticismo," in *Questioni e correnti di storia letteraria* (Milano, 1965), p. 641.

of the usually short-lived, superfluous and torrid love affairs that are so indigenous to this society. The particular effect of these adjectives is further substantiated by the fact that *Storia di una capinera*, a novel that deals with an altogether different theme and society, is practically devoid of such terms.

3.1.7. Many of the nouns that, by their figurative and emotive power, contribute, like the above adjectives, to the display of these characters' passionate mood are likewise of rare occurrence in the standard language. The following is an examplary list arranged in order of progressive intensity: *sensazione* (98, 111), *palpito* (259), *effusione* (96), *pulsazione* (101), *anelito* (308, 315), *ardore* (225), *fascino* (10, 48, 62, 90, 262, 276, 373, et al.), *esaltazione* (102, 237, 311), *passione* (95, 102, 106), *voluttà* (32, 43, 53, 68, 88, 90, 91, 121, 337, 339), *ebbrezza* (243, 254, 262), *delirio* (107, 117, 121), *parossismo* (48, 51, 105, 117), *spasimo* (90, 117, 313), *agonia* (109, 110, 111, 126, 127).

3.1.8. There are also instances, especially at the beginning of this period, where Verga, without ever stepping outside of that social norm, will adopt terms of a more learned nature in order to conceal what he might have deemed regional forms. The literary *verone* (18, 29, 32, 33, 35, 37, 45, 88, et al.), a term virtually unknown in Southern Italy, is preferred to the more common *balcone*;[9] *sentire* is often replaced by the more archaic *udire* ("l'ha *udito* dunque" -16, "Il rumore [...] si fece *udire* da lontano " -49, "*udì* aprire la porta" -41, "Pietro *udì* il passo leggero" -49, et al.); the more conventional *portare* often yelds to *recare* ("che sa *recare* con grazia" -32, "colla doppia chiave che *recava* sempre addosso" -52) and to *arrecare* ("la contrarietà che gli *arrecava* quella domanda" -30, "Il freddo mi *arrecava* convulsioni" -289); *attendere* is sometimes found in place of *aspettare* ("non dia più occasione ad *attendermi* domani" -45) and *rammentare* in place of *ricordare* ("non *rammento*" -E.73, "Ho bisogno di *rammentarle* i nostri patti" -E.106). *Motto* and *verbo* are favorite substitutes for the more common *parola* in negative statements ("non disse *motto*" -E.12, "senze dir *motto*" -256, E.66, E.132, "senza far *motto*" -251, 297,

---

[9] Cf. Russo, *Verga,* p. 285.

"non disse *verbo*" -E.73) and *motteggiare* and *ciarlare* appear along with the more common *parlare* and *chiacchierare* ("Anche *motteggiando* aveva di queste lugubri allusioni" -340, "*Ciarlami* un po' di tutto" -138, "Vorrei *ciarlare* con te" -195, "a fumare e a *ciarlare* di donne" -361, "dopo aver *ciarlato* ancora una mezz'ora" -368, "andarono sui bastioni in carrozza, *ciarlando*, fumando" -E.120).

3.1.9. The rather large selection of foreign terms present in these pages has also to be considered as an integral part of the norm belonging to this drawing-room society. As would be expected, the majority of these terms are of French origin [10] and are associated primarily with the world of fashion: "le donne che sappiano recare così bene il loro *pardessus reine blanche*" (22), "quel briccone in guanti paglia e *pincenez*" (22), "abito di *tarlatane*" (27), "cappellino grigio ornato *cerise*" (27), "veste di seta *granadine*" (39), "il *bóurnous* che le copriva le spalle" (39), *bóurnous* bianco sulle spalle" (97), "mantelletta Fatma di peluscio" (60), "*vespertina* di *cachemire* bianco" (70), "il *fisciù* alitava lieve lieve" (E.47), "gli sgonfietti del *fisciù*" (E.99). In addition: *duchesse* (110), *réclame* (241), *buffet* (300, 301), *cotillon* (342, E.46), *canapè* (346, E.10, E.29, E.104, E.106, et al.), *dessert* (E.111), *bosse* ("ha la *bosse* del matrimonio" -E.85), *schicche* (E.86, E.120), *étagère* (E.103). Some scattered French phrases and various anglicisms are also intended to show the usual linguistic versality and finesse of expression of such a society: "*En place pour la quadrille!*" (36), *un peu, beaucoup, passionnément — passionnément! — Mais non! rien du tout!* (333), "*Souvent femme varie!*" (E.112); *dandys* (15), *revolver* (62, 381), *ponce* (281), *spleen* (356, E.150), *plaid* (E.152).

3.1.10. Many of the foreign entries are included in the long list of carriage designations found in these works. As Migliorini points out, the nomenclature for the carriage is in itself another extension of the mannerisms of a society such as this and the leaning toward the use of foreign terms — primarily French and

---

[10] B. Migliorini points out in the chapter on the 19th Cent. of his *Storia,* that Italian culture was heavily influenced by the French and many of the French forms had been adopted by the Italian bourgeois.

English — is identifiable, more specifically and chronologically, with the *bon ton* that the author is delineating. [11]

3.1.10a. Among the carriages for hire, *fiacre* (228, 246, 260, 335, E.98, E.121), used for travel within the city, and *coupè* (E.152), used for longer trips, are held in higher favor than the more ordinary *carrozza da nolo* ("modesta *carrozza da nolo*" -9).

3.1.10b. The list of elegant carriages, however, is much more extensive. *Carrozza* and *legno,* although used at times in their more general sense, also preserve a more specialized meaning, either directly or by way of reference to a previously mentioned carriage belonging to this group. For examples with *carrozza* see pp. 10, 228, 229, 326, 340, E.87, E.120, E.121, et al. and for *legno* see pp. 228, 246, E.98, et al. Also found are *legnetto* ("un elegante *legnetto*" -228; also 247), *calesse* ("un elegante *calesse* signorile" -9, "il *calesse* ci seguì" -103), *calèche* ("distesa mollemente nella superba *calèche*" -E.88, "la *calèche* era ovattata, riboccante di fiori" -E.143; see also E.142, E.144), *phaéton* ("troneggiava dai quattro cuscini del suo *phaéton*" -E.86; also E.144), *brougham* (E.120) and *equipaggio* ("brillante *equipaggio*" -11). To the more luxurious class belong *daumont* ("la sfolgorante *daumont*" -E.87) and *cocchio* ("la promessa che faceva scendere la dea dal suo *cocchio* suberbo" -227, "di quel tal *cocchio* che lo menava attraverso la giovinezza allegramente" -321).

3.1.10c. Still with reference to carriages, the preference for foreign terms extends at times to the men that tend to horses: *jockey* (70, E.143), *groom* (E.144, E.146).

3.1.11. The mannerisms of this society are further reflected through their preferred type of entertainment and their cultural interests. Aside from an occasional *cotillon* and *quadrille,* this society dances almost exclusively to the rhythm of the waltz and sometimes the waltz also carries emotive and evocative strengths. In *Una peccatrice,* for example, the waltz contributes to Pietro's infatuation for Narcisa: he hears her play "un valtzer allora in

---

[11] Migliorini, *Storia,* p. 664 in particular.

gran voga: *Il Bacio* di Arditi" (49) and from then on it will contribute to their pains and joys, until Narcisa's death. Pietro and Narcisa will always react emotionally to "*Il Bacio* di Arditi" (see, for ex., pp. 51, 68, 69, 96) and her last wish before dying will be that of wanting to hear for the last time the waltz that has by now become theirs (see pp. 122, 125, 126). It is also in *Una peccatrice* that Verga makes a distinction in social levels through the type of dance that is preferred. While the waltz is one of the "balli aristocratici" (61), the polka (*La Fasola*) is best suited to the lower class (see pp. 54-62).

3.1.12. In addition to the aformentioned "*Bacio* di Arditi," there are several other references made to cultural productions. Most popular are the musical compositions. Verdi's *La Traviata* (20), *Ernani* (49), *Don Carlos* (338) and *Un ballo in maschera* (E.62) are mentioned; "le più appassionate melodie di Bellini e Verdi" (26) are appreciated just as much as "il duetto del *Ruy-Blas*" (353) and Schubert's *Addio* (E.104) and his other songs (E.50). Also not forgotten are the compositions of Liszt (E.59) and Strauss (E.45). As for literature, a certain "volume di Prati" (323, 371), certainly *Edmenegarda,* is of sentimental importance.

3.2.1. Present also several allusions of a historico-literary nature. These allusions, in addition to contributing to the depiction of the cultural level of the world being described, also give a very significant indication of one of Verga's most basic and lasting modes of presentation. The reader will immediately notice that these allusions are almost always used in a comparative sense — very often, in fact, they are preceded by *come* or its equivalents — to denote a particular physical or mental attitude of the characters. This device of allusion, seen within the context of this society's cultural and mental behavior, comes to serve a function similar to that of the nicknames in the mature works. If, in the latter case, nicknames are the result of an associative process based on the limited level of consciousness of a primitive society whose roots lie very much within the local folklore and whose vision is always in direct connection with the physical objects surrounding them, in the former case it is the cultural reservoir that provides much of the associative material.

3.2.2. The following examples will clarify what has been stated above. Pietro Brusio is "orgoglioso come *un Cid*" (17) and, at one of his vocal outbursts, he is told by his friend Raimondo: "Come ti hanno guastato i romanzi di Sue; tu accanito avversario dell' esagerazione della scuola francese, e che ora mi copii sì bravamente l'uomo stufo a vent'anni, *lo Scipione* del *Martino il Trovatello*..." (19). Dumas' heroine is clearly in the author's mind when Narcisa is referred to as "*Margherita* dell'aristocrazia" (10) and it is not coincidental that, later, Pietro describes one of his old flames by citing Verdi's *Traviata*: "In seguito amai una fanciulla ... pura siccome un angiolo, come direbbe il signor Germont nella *Traviata*" (20). On one occasion in *Tigre reale* Giorgio recollects a night spent with Nata as "l'ultima sera che abbiamo passato insieme giocando a Giulietta e Romeo" (347). In *Eros,* Alberto's passion and way of acting earn him a comparison with Foscolo's *Jacopo Ortis* ("era sopraggiunto il carnevale, e il giovane *Ortis* non s'era fatto scrupolo di andare ad un veglione" -68) and in his momentary indecision at to whether or not he should go to Adele's window, "esitò alcuni istanti, come ogni *Cesare* che stia per passare il Rubicone" (33). Biblical allusions are made by Raimondo, in *Una peccatrice,* when he tells Pietro: "Ho guardato ma non ho visto, come il cieco della Bibbia" (21) and by Alberto, in *Eros,* when he claims that his latest lover would love him even if he were "povero come *Giobbe*" (E.101). An allusion to the popular legend is also made to Alberto when, as a result of his constant and tiresome wanderings throughout the world, he is compared to l'Ebreo Errante" (E.141). In addition to a stock allusion to the figure of Cato ("saresti il *Catone* del momento" -30), a mythological reference is also used in giving a satirical description of one of the characters: "Il principe (. . .) Metelliani (. . .) troneggiava (. . .) come un *Apollo brutto*" (E.86.). It is quite consonant with the clerical atmosphere of *Storia di una capinera* that Maria would think, in one instance, of writing to her friend: "Tu riderai di me, e mi darai del *Sant'Agostino in gonnella*" (137).

3.2.3. There is also a good number of cases where the nicknames — often italicized — are of a more indigenous nature since they are formulated more directly by the characters. This observation has to be viewed as a clearer indication of Verga's increasing propensity for the adoption of the nickname device. Narcisa, since she comes from Piedmont, is also known as *la Piemontese*: "vedevano *la Piemontese,* come l'aveva soprannominata Raimondo" (33, and also 31, 34); Maddalena, one of Pietro's early loves, is also known as *la piccina*: "ci credi nel serio (...) che Maddalena, *la piccina,* come la chiami, pianga" (18, and also 23); a whole group refers to one of their acquaintances as *Alfonso il bello*: "Sai Alfonso? *Alfonso il bello?* è proprio una disgrazia!" (362). Velleda and Adele, because of their countenance, are called *la principessa* and *Elisabetta d'Inghilterra* respectively: "con quell'altera indifferenza che l'avea fatta soprannominare *la principessa*" (E.39), "Ella portava alta la testa (...) e uno sguardo profondo che l'avevano fatta soprannominare *Elisabetta d'Inghilterra*" (E.142). Countess Armandi is also known as *la bella toscana* ("era stato suo amico, a della marchesa, ch'era datta a Milano *la bella toscana*" -E.122) and Alberto, known to many as il *figliuolo della marchesa Alberti* ("certi forestieri che visitavano il collegio avevano mostrato di conoscerlo come il *figliuolo della marchesa Alberti*" -E.13), is called by her Milanese friend Selene *biondino* (Mi chiama *biondino*" -E.101, "To! eri tu, *biondino?*" -E.119). On one occasion a dialect term stands for a nickname. Enrico Lanti presents himself to the narrator by reminding him that they had been to school together as children and that at that time he (Enrico), because of his short size, roundness and jovial aspect, was known as *badduzza*: "Io ero così grosso che mi chiamavano *badduzza*; ti rammenti?" (232).

3.2.4.　Certain phrases that although not really nicknames function as such are also worthy of considerations. These expressions, through their constant repetition, tend to emphasize particular descriptive aspects of a character. Think of Don Michele, in the *Malavoglia,* always described as carrying his gun on his stomach and with his pants tucked in his boots. In *Eros,* there is Alberto's uncle who rubs his hands whenever things go as planned and in his favor (see 15, 18). In *Eva,* the author focuses considerable attention on a doctor for whom he seems to have a great deal of respect: "Il chirurgo — un nostro carissimo amico, molto conosciuto a Mentana come il *Dottore dal cappello bianco* — esaminò la ferita" (306), "Il *Dottore dal cappello bianco* s'inginocchiò presso del conte" (307).

3.3.1. The inclination that Verga will have toward the use of proverbs is already somewhat in evidence in these pages. Although here the proverbs are neither many nor do they possess the deep spiritual meaning and rigorousness of *I Malavoglia,* they are nonetheless indicative of the author's future path and they do have for the characters a function quite similar to that of the characters in his masterpiece. Making a marginal observation of a more strictly psychological nature, it is apparent that, in *Una peccatrice,* Pietro's failure becomes a reality when he pays no heed to his own sayings: "vi è un detto celebre: *Fumo di gloria non val fumo di pipa:* (. . .) io ne faccio un altro: Amor di donna, e d'uomo, se si vuole, non dura più di cenere di carta o di biglietto amoroso . . . o sigaro regalia" (21). Regardless of these self-warnings, Pietro will allow himself to fall madly, even if briefly, in love with Narcisa and he also lets himself be carried away with his short-lived theatrical success. The proverbs, as padron 'Ntoni will later state, never deceive. "Ogni proverbio, per chi lo ripete con intima adesione, è ab eterno" [12] and he who does not follow it is destined to fail. Pietro is no exception.

3.4.1. The Tuscan and Florentine influence becomes increasingly evident throughout this period. While at first Verga is affected primarily by single terms he will, later, adopt phrases and expressions and handle them with considerable ease. The Tuscan influence not only reveals Verga's inclination to adopt an expression deemed as the norm that came closest to that of the written language but also demonstrates his interest — since many of the expressions derive from the spoken norm — in dealing with the living language of the time. [13]

---

[12] A. Cirese, "I proverbi nei *Malavoglia,*" in *Pagine di critica letteraria,* ed. Acrosso (Palermo, 1962), III, 230.

[13] Three major sources have been consulted in the examination of the Tuscan and Florentine element: Rigutini and Fanfani, *Vocabolario italiano della lingua parlata,* 2nd ed. (Firenze, 1893), Tommaseo and Bellini, *Dizionario della lingua italiana,* 3rd ed. (Torino, 1924), P. Fanfani, *Vocabolario dell'uso toscano* (Firenze, 1863).

3.4.2. In addition to examples such as the many *-ino* ending terms (see sec. 3.1.4., 3.1.4a., 3.1.4b.) and to the exclamatory statements starting with *O* (see sec. 2.10.4.), of clear derivation from the spoken Tuscan and Florentine are forms such as *babbo* (135, 143, 149, 150, 165, 179, 185, 189, 199, 202, 322, 359, E.13, E.14, E.15, E.18, et al.), [14] *baloccarsi* (367), *bambi* (131), *bamboccio* (360, 369, 371), *bisbetica* (E.107), *briciolo* ("senza fare un *briciolo* di corte" -334), *cospetto* (21), *ciao* (E.69, E.70), *maluccio* ("stava *maluccio*" -374), *marmocchio* (360), *ninnoli* (E.91), *stampo* ("non son fatto del loro *stampo*" -38), *superbietta* ("rispose Alberto con un po' di *superbietta* ... da geloso" E.85), *vagheggino* ("punta dal freddo del suo *vagheggino*" -70).

3.4.3. Tuscan and Florentine flavor is also sensed in the following phrases and expressions: "*N'è* vero?" (334), *pagare lo scotto* (55), *fare buon viso* (67), *far furore* (69), "le *devamo la berta*" (134), "Salta a *piè pari* questo periodo sul quale *tiro una bella croce*" (135), "*buscarmi* da te *una ramanzina*" (149), "tu forse sapresti *trovarci il bandolo!*" (153), "Ci offri *da cena*" (230), "*tiene il sacco* all'adulterio" (311), "si specchiavano *facendo boccacce* nella vernice" (322; also 356), *montargli la testa* (324, 342, E.134), "la lista dei balli era *piena zeppa*" (325), "Giorgio aveva *tenuto il letto*" (326), "le so *punta testa*" (328), "girar la testa *come una trottola*" (334), *darsi bel tempo* (335), *in fede mia* (362), "lo *mena pel naso*" (362), "è stata lei che *l'ha piantato*" (364), *la scapperemo bella* (411), "si fosse *mescolato della bisogna*" (E.13), *giocare a volano* (E.14, E.15) "*montare la mosca* al naso" (E.15), *fare le viste* (E.19, et al.), "il dialogo (...) si *reggeva sui trampoli*" (E.21), *menare il can per l'aia* (E.34), *fare i mirallegro* (E.51, et al.) *andare in collera* (E.59), "*a mo'* di" (E.66, E.156, et al.), "aver *corso la cavallina* in gioventù" (E.122), "avea *fatto giudizio*" (E.134), "stette dinanzi a quel letto *lunga pezza*" (E.189).

3.5.1. For as much as Verga may have tried, during this period, to divest himself of the Southern norm and of the Sicilian element in particular, he was never able — and quite naturally — to do so completely. Even if he did not resort to the Sicilian dialect, he was

---

[14] This lexeme will continue to appear in Verga's mature works.

unable to keep away from certain terms and expressions that clearly point to his provenience. [15]

3.5.2. Russo points out that the word *immondezze* ("non rischio più di farmi gettare delle *immondezze*" -18), for example, is the italianized form of a term predominantly used in the South and not in the North and the expression "La bella donna!" (15), used to show surprise and enchantment at the incomparable beauty of a woman seen passing by, is also an abstract and arbitrary translation from the Sicilian dialect. [16] Associated with the Sicilian dialect are also *manco male* (369) and the use of *musica* ("*la musica* eseguiva le più appassionate melodie" -26, "*la musica* eseguiva *il Bacio* di Arditi" -68) in place of the more normal *orchestra*.

3.5.3. In most cases, however, rather than with the single terms, the intimation of a Southern, if not strictly Sicilian, flavor lies within the context of phrases which are often accountable for the relatively few happy expressive moments of these novels; "io l'ucciderò, *com'è vero che* mi chiamo Pietro" (72-73), "Te lo *giuro sul mio onore*" (177), "*In parola d'onore* (...) metterò tanto di catenaccio alla porta di casa!" (361) (these expressions that reflect the Sicilian sense of honor bring to mind future works such as "Cavalleria rusticana" and "La Lupa"), "si sarebbe detta una donna *tutta miele* dai capelli alla bocca" (E.60), "E che Pietro (...) è *innamorato cotto*" (34), "*prende* un bagno" (36), "avea *fatto giudizio*" (E.134), "E *di buona razza*" (E.120). The various expressions denoting surprise and containing *occhi* and more particularly the phrase *tanto d'occhi* might be more directly attributed to the Sicilian norm: "Ascoltava la mamma con *tanto d'occhi* aperti" (367), "avea spalancato *tanto d'occhi* a quella sfuriata" (E.26), "Adele spalancò *tanto d'occhi*" (E.29), "c'era rimasto a guardare con *tanto d'occhi* spalancati" (E.69), "con *occhi* neri grandi così" (341).

---

[15] The following sources have been consulted in the examination of the Sicilian element: A. Traina, *Nuovo vocabolario siciliano-italiano,* 2nd ed. (Palermo, 1890), A. Traina, *Vocabolarietto delle voci siciliane* (Palermo, 1888), V. Mortillaro, *Nuovo dizionario siciliano-italiano* (Palermo, 1838-1844) and revised edition (Palermo, 1876).

[16] *Verga,* pp. 285-86.

3.6.1. Except for the Sicilian *badduzza,* adopted as a nickname (see sec. 3.2.3), Verga never resorts to orthographically presented dialectal forms [17] but in *Eros* there are some lexemes that, although presented in the standardized Italian, are clear derivatives of the Milanese dialect: "Sono innamorato (...) di una bella *tosa* che avevo conosciuta" (101), "Ella m'insegna un po' di *meneghino,* così ci perfezioniamo a vicenda" (102). The leaning toward the adoption of these terms — however slight it may be — is of significant importance for it gives a clearer glimpse of the "verismo" narrative that is to come.

3.7.1. Of noticeable importance are certain locutions and images that, because of their recurrent appearance and the special treatment that the author gives them, become rather conspicuous.

3.7.2. To describe someone (or something) that is still a tyro — not yet adept at his profession — Verga prefers to use the expression *in erba.* This phrase appears at least once in every novel: "dimostrerebbe che le mie più belle *produzioni-erba* non valgono il fumo delizioso di questo regalia" (21), "È una *celebrità in erba,* dunque?" (65), "Ero un *genio in erba,* una speranza dell' arte italiana" (235), "In tutta la sera non riuscì al *diplomatico in erba* di attirare l'attenzione della contessa" (329), "sono un povero diavolo di *medico in erba*" (E.52).

3.7.3. Verga must have also been very happy with his handling of the *farfalla-bruco* image, which appears for the first time in *Una peccatrice* ("Io amo [...] in lei questa toletta, questo lusso, questo apparato brillante e vaporoso in cui la *farfalla* mi fa dimenticare il *bruco*" -35) but comes to assume much greater proportions in *Eva*: "La *farfalla* tornava *bruco,* ed io ne risentivo un dispetto ed una amarezza indicibili" (243). In this last case this image will function pivotally and its presence will be felt, in one sense or another, throughout the entire story. [18]

---

[17] T. G. Bergin, in his *Giovanni Verga* (New Haven, 1931), p. 22, notes, in fact, that "badduzza" and "ntuppatedda" (this last term appears in *Novelle Milanesi*) are the only Sicilian dialect terms appearing in Verga's early production.

[18] This image will be, in other words, a constant reminder of Eva's dual aspect: on one side will lie the true Eva, the frank, open and honest woman

3.7.4. Close attention should be accorded to *fare della musica,* a locution considered by the purists unpleasant and therefore not totally acceptable. [19] It appears first in *Una peccatrice* and once in *Storia di una capinera.* However, it occurs more frequently in *Eros* and the purpose of its use appears to be radically different between the first two novels and the last one. While its appearance in the first novels may be attributed primarily to the author's still amateurish approach to the affected speech patterns of the society he is describing ("La sera *facevamo della musica* insieme" -92, "Dopo *si fece un po' di musica*" -148), in *Eros* this expression is adopted with full cognizance of its unattractiveness. The author feels justified in using it since what he intends to display through this linguistically distasteful phrase is — and here we are entering into the psychological and stylistic sphere — his own distaste for the behavior of this affected society. The ironic and double meaning of this phrase becomes very clear when one considers it within its context. In an invitation to Alberto, countess Armandi writes: "verrete domani alle quattro? Avrò anche la signora Rigalli, e *faremo della musica*" (110). Not much later the same phrase appears again, but this time with a more pungent and suggestive tone: "La contessa riceveva Alberti frequentemente di giorno (...) e di sera, allorchè *faceva della musica*: il marchese era distinto pianista, e l'Armandi amava la musica appassionatamente — ognuno lo sapeva" (116). In another instance, to Alberti's "Non avevo altro da dirvi" countess Armandi replies with the sarcasm of a betrayed lover: "Nemmeno che avreste *fatto della musica* colla signora Rigalli (...). Non è così?" (114). This expression reaches its culminating point in a dialogue between Count Armandi and his wife. Having reasons to suspect her fidelity, he asks her if Alberto had paid her a visit and noticing a tone of apprehension in her affirmative reply he somewhat mockingly adds: "Avete *fatto della musica*?" To this — and here the author is openly sardonic — she counters: "Pochissimo; non mi sentivo bene. Ho un po' di mal di capo..." (129).

---

that she really is; on the other side the false Eva that Enrico Lanti and others want to see.

[19] Cf. E. Treves, *...Si dice?...,* 4th ed. (Milano, 1961), p. 190 and also Palazzi, *Novissimo dizionario.*

3.8.1. Some of the themes and literary expedients destined to occupy a special place in Verga's future production are already present here; some still appear in a rather unsettled fashion while others are already well consolidated.

3.8.2. The family theme is undoubtedly one of the themes that comes to occupy an increasingly strong position. Its presence is well in evidence in each of the novels and its role is of growing importance.

3.8.2a. In *Una peccatrice,* the importance placed on the family is reflected in Pietro's tender attitude and almost reverential respect for his mother. He speaks to and of his mother in a tone of awe, almost as if he were praying: "Pietro amava sua madre d'immenso affetto" (25), "Grazie, grazie, buona madre! ... " (47). "Madre mia! (...) ti chiedo perdono di quello che ho detto e fatto" (46), "Perdonami, madre mia! ... perdonami!" (64), et al.

3.8.2b. In *Storia di una capinera* this theme is approached more openly and directly. It seems, in fact, that this work sets the ground for the future works. Through the protagonist's behavior and statements, the author is clearly trying to establish the importance that he places on the family as an institution. In the works that follow, instead, his interest will be focused on the inner function of the family and its members. Here, the author, like Maria, whose tragedy is caused at least in part by her family's unwillingness to take her into its bosom, sees the family as an outsider looking in while in the future works the family will be viewed from a different angle: fewer generalizations and more direct and intrinsic interest in its function.

In this novel there are many notes that reveal the importance, sacredness and comfort of the "focolare domestico" (and *domestico* is indeed one of the key words used in reference to the family):

> ... mi pare che cotesta *famigliuola* (...) debba amarsi dippiù ed essere maggiormente felice; mi pare che tutte quelle affezioni, circoscritte fra *quelle pareti*, debbano essere più intime, più complete. (136-37)

> ... se queste gioie fossero un peccato! se il Signore si sdegnasse di vedermi preferire al convento (...) la campagna, l'aria libera, *la famiglia*! ... (137)

la famiglia è una benedizione del cielo! (140)

come se si restringessero i legami che mi uniscono ai miei
cari nell'*intimità della vita domestica.* (140)

Sai com'è piacevole (...) quel lume ospitale che ci guida (...), che ci fe pensare alle *pareti domestiche* e a tutte
le *tranquille contentezze della famiglia*? (145)

Ho perduto anche la consolazione della famiglia. (...)
L'intimità domestica sparisce. (184)

Penso a mio padre, alla *mia famigliuola,* a tutte le cose
che addolcirebbero (...) le presenti sofferenze. (197)

nella sua vita, nel suo affetto, tutte le *serenità della pace,*
tutte *le benedizioni della famiglia.* (213)

3.8.2c. In *Eva,* this motif functions as a counterbalancing force
to Enrico's drama. In the most difficult and dramatic moments of
his emotional distress, the thought of the family seems to calm him
somewhat. The family, when opposed to the "atmosfera di Banche
e di imprese industriali," (225) plays for the protagonist a redemp-
tive role. It is seen, in other words, as the antagonist of that vitiated
society that Enrico has allowed himself to fall victim to. The family
constitutes the main block of the world free of "rettorica" and
"ipocrisie" (cf. 225) and it will, eventually, win over its opponent.
It is the thought and the strength of the family that will bring Enrico
back, even if a little late, on the right track. In no other novel has
the author been so decisively clear in establishing such a contrast. The emphasis on the family becomes clear from the very
first pages. Enrico, however weak and hollow he may appear
throughout the story, is touching whenever he speaks of the family:

> Conosci la mia famiglia? ... La conoscerai, (...) son brava
> gente; non son signori, ma portrai stringer loro la mano
> francamente (...) e parlar di me (...). La mia povera
> mamma piangerebbe anche la perdita della anima mia ...
> (232-33)

And later:

> Ma non penso a ciò che per i miei genitori, e per la mia
> sorellina ... Stringendo la tua mano mi sembra di strin-

germi al cuore quei poveretti che saranno tanti afflitti ...
Ecco perchè ho voluto parlarti. Non è vero che in certi
momenti, quando siamo lontani dalla famiglia, proviamo
delle strane tenerezze per le persone che ce la rammen-
tano, o che hanno il più lontano rapporto con essa?
(233-34)

He further adds:

Se tu sapessi come son fatti gli occhi della madre che ti
affissano in volto in certi momenti e ti chiedono certe cose!
(234)

These statements serve to heighten the dramatic impact later,
when Enrico finds it necessary to financially exploit his family in
order to satisfy his whims. The sacred respect that he apparently
has for the family does not hinder, at least temporarily, his im-
pudent requests:

Vorrei credere che fossi pazzo, perchè fui assai vigliacco,
perchè fui infame. Io divenni esigente sino all'impossibile
verso la mia povera famiglia — fino a strapparle il necessario per comprarmi delle cravatte. Non scrivevo altro che
per chieder danaro, e mentivo anche l'affezione! Oh, mia
povera mamma! Oh, padre mio! ... e non arrossivo allorchè vedevo giungere quel danaro che costava tanti stenti
ai miei genitori! No! non arrossivo! (263-64)

3.8.2d. In *Tigre reale* and *Eros* the family theme achieves the
position of "un'etica superiore"[20] and it is no longer "in apparenza
ma nella sostanza, più profondamente inserito nella logica del racconto, al cui fondo esso rimane legato e riflesso."[21] In both stories
the main characters, namely Giorgio La Ferlita and Alberto Alberti, are faced with the choice of pursuing, on one side, the life
of that chimerical and mundane society into which they were born
and that is basically hollow and lacking in true human sentiments
and, on the other side, that morally wholesome life provided by
the family. In both cases the family comes out the winner; Giorgio
abandons Nata to return to his wife and child and Alberto chooses

---

[20] R. Luperini, *Pessimismo e verismo in Giovanni Verga*, p. 32.
[21] C. Musumarra, *Verga minore*, p. 106.

to take his own life rather than returning to his old vitiated way
of life when he realizes that he has not been able to live up to
and to reciprocate his wife's unscathed love and affection. The
phrases that allude to the serenity, happiness and candor of the family and of its members, to the atmosphere that surrounds them
and to the impact that these various factors have on some of the
characters, are numerous in these novels too:

> la nostra felicità (that of the family) non ci costa nulla,
> è facile, semplice e tranquilla. (363)

> Giorgio avea guardato la moglie con tutti altri occhi. Le
> scopriva ogni giorno di più un'attrattiva pudica, velata (...)
> negli occhi limpidi, nell'accento carezzevole, nell'attitudine
> modesta (...) coteste qualità la rendevano più leggiadra;
> sentiva che se non fosse stato suo marito, la seduzione di
> quella grazia così schietta, così ingenua e riservata, avrebbe
> acceso sino al furore i suoi desiderî di seduttore stanco
> e noiato di artificî donneschi.... Ed era strano che
> quell'uomo amasse per la prima volta sua moglie. (399)

> l'immagine di sua moglie, di suo figlio infermo, della sua
> dimora tranquilla, della sua *felicità domestica,* mischiavasi
> a quel fantasma della donna. (384)

> Una delle sofferenze più acerbe che sentisse era il supplizio
> di dover stare una mezz'ora al cospetto della moglie, di
> dover incontrare lo sguardo limpido di lei, e ascoltare la
> sua voce inalterabilmente dolce e calma. Quella camera
> avea una fisonimia onesta; l'aria sembrava circolarvi pura
> e libera (...) — avea un che d'augusto. (398)

> sembrava che quelle *pareti domestiche* lo circondassero,
> lo abbracciassero quasi, per proteggerlo e per difenderlo.
> (408)

> Possedeva tutte le disgrazie; l'immaginazione calda, l'in-
> dole fiacca, il cuore sensibilissimo, ma non temprato da
> *affetti domestici.* (E.138)

> Ammogliatevi! (...) La famiglia vi salverebbe.... So quel
> che vuol dire essere soli al mondo! (E.150)

> Quella vita calma e serena (with respect to Alberto's
> marriage to Adele), circoscritta in un orizzonte limitato,
> confacevasi alla stanchezza dell'animo suo, e al bisogno
> che provava di rinascere in quell'amore così nuovo, sen-

za che altre immagini del passato potessero venire a tur-
bare il suo pensiero ed a mettere in pericolo quell'intimità
che gli faceva tanto bene. (E.158)

3.8.2e. The frequency with which the references to the family
appear and the importance given to them leave no doubt that the
family theme stands out as the common denominator of Verga's
moral and poetic world and as such it acquires the proportions
of a "tema-mito." [22] It "sopravvive" to use Terracini's words, "al
di là del momento espressivo da cui è fiorito, ed assume nella
coscienza del poeta una vita autonoma, è un elemento, capace di
evocare per lui tutto il mondo dal quale è fuoruscito." [23] The future
works will testify to this even more.

3.8.3. References to the *destino* theme are also in evidence in
these pages but, unlike the family theme, it is still far from having
the deep and inherent meaning of the later phase. Although it is
used primarily in a formalistic way it does give proof, nonetheless,
of the author's interest in its use: "se tu fossi *destinato* ad amare
quella donna, che non hai veduto che due volte, in passando? ..."
(25), "immaginiamoci che per un capriccio, una fantasia, *un destino,*
secondo te, questa donna si innamori di te" (30), "voi siete la
vittima della vostra posizione, della cattiveria di vostra matrigna,
della debolezza di vostro padre, del *destino!*" (167), "Vanità,
curiosità, simpatia fisica, non importa, — c'era l'*ignoto* dentro —
il gran dio" (323), "Dopo vent'anni che non s'erano più visti Alberto e sua cugina s'incontrarono a Firenze, spinti dal *turgine della
fatalità*" (E.142).

3.8.3a. Much more significant and prophetic, however, is one
statement that the author puts into the mouth of one of his prota-
gonists:

> *Destino!* ecco la gran parola che gli uomini non sanno
> proferire più spesso, ma nella quale io son credente come
> un maomettano (...). Se gli uomini sapessero far valere
> questa parola quanto essa lo merita, l'incolpabilità delle
> azioni umane rimarrebbe sugli scritti dei penalisti. (24)

---

[22] See B. Terracini, *Analisi stilistica,* p. 35.
[23] Terracini, *Analisi,* p. 35.

As trite and conventional as this phrase may sound on the lips
of Pietro Brusio, it will soon come to acquire — to paraphrase
Russo — a much deeper inflexion and resonance in the world of
"Nedda" and of *I Malavoglia*. [24] This phrase shows that the tragic
fatalism that will weigh on Verga's future cosmos is already present,
even though muted.

3.8.4. The fondness that Verga will display for animal metaphors and analogies in his later works is already in evidence here.
This fondness is already suggested by some of the titles but it
will become most apparent primarily in the description of the
behavioristic attitude of some of the female characters.

3.8.4a. In *Storia di una capinera*, the title itself suggests "un
tacito confronto con la protagonista." [25] In the introduction, with his
explanation of how he has decided on the title (see p. 132), Verga
gives clear indications of the analogy that he wishes to draw
between the suffering of his characters and the arduous perseverance
of some of these animals. This can also be said of *Tigre reale*. This
relationship immediately brings to mind the many implicit and
explicit animal analogies found in his mature works and particularly in the various stories of *Novelle rusticane* and *Vita dei Campi*
(i.e., "Jeli il pastore," "L'asino di San Giuseppe," "Rosso Malpelo"
and others). In addition, Verga also introduces, with these titles,
another feature that he will later favor. The observation made by
Chiappelli in his study of "La Lupa" [26] can very well be applied to
these novels that are given animal titles. As in that short story, here
too it appears that "la narrativa scaturisce ... dal fantasma del personaggio" and that "l'icasticità della figura" [27] supplies both the title
and the leit-motif of the story.

3.8.4b. The animal-associated images applied to women cover
a wide gamut of human sentiments ranging from tenderness and
coquettishness to outright passion and madness. In *Eros*, for exam-

---

[24] *Verga*, p. 36.

[25] Russo, *Verga*, p. 291.

[26] "Una lettura verghiana: 'La Lupa'," *Giornale storico della letteratura
italiana*, 139 (1962), 370-83.

[27] Chiappelli, "Lettura verghiana," p. 370.

ple, Adele's innocence, kindness and shyness are all implied in the word *cerbiatta*, to which she is compared when, while talking to Alberto, she hears her father's cough: "Adele scappò come una *cerbiatta* spaventata" (37). When Velleda is compared to a *cerbiatta* however, something totally different is implied. In this second case *cerbiatta* stands for a beautiful and graceful animal who lures its admirers with its flirtatious attitude: "Velleda stava presso il pianoforte (. . .) come una *cerbiatta* attorniata da una muta di cani; ma la *cerbiatta* teneva testa da tutte le parti, col brio, col sorriso, colla parola" (45).

In other instances, one finds that the piercing glances and the movements of these sensuous women are often compared to those of a wild feline; "Ella aveva i capelli sciolti, e me ne sferzava il viso con certi *movimenti felini*" (261), "nella *pupilla felina* corruscavano delle bramosie indefinite ed ardenti" (326), "lo scostava per fissargli uno *sguardo felino* negli occhi senza dire una parola" (381), "i movimenti di lei avevano certa *elasticità* carezzevole e *felina*; — accanto a ciò una *timidità* quasi *selvaggia*" (E.17), "uscì con un *movimento felino*" (E.84), "arrovesciò il capo all'indietro (. . .) con un *movimento felino*" (E.115). Their passionate thirst and reaction to unfulfilled desires are occasionally described, in addition to *leonessa* (see sec. 3.1.2e.), with the help of terms such as *tigre* ("ho urlato come una *tigre*" -120), *lupa* ("l'avvinse in un abbraccio da *lupa*" -381) and *natura selvaggia* ("Cotesta donna avea tutte le avidità, tutti i capricci, tutte le sazietà, tutte le impazienze nervose di una *natura selvaggia*" -326).

3.8.4c. Storia di una capinera deserves a closer look. Here Verga is able to blend masterfully the tender affection that Maria exhibits for small animals at the beginning of the story with her own subsequent deranged animal-like behavior. Words such as *uccelletti, lodolette, farfallette* give way to animalistic metaphors and to much stronger animal-associated locutions that are employed to delineate her passionate desires, anger and eventual madness: "l'angoscia mi divora come un *cane rabbioso*" (176), "Invento anche dei peccati (. . .) che mi nascondo gelosamente nel cuore *come una lupa* nasconde i suoi figli nell'antro" (204), "vorrei urlare *come una belva*" (204), "andremo a nasconderci nel castagneto . . . soli . . . *come le belve*" (217), "vorrei essere *tigre*! (. . .) vorrei *strapparmi a brani* queste carni" (207), "sono andata a rintanarmi nella mia cella come una *belva* ferita" (212), "son *belva!* son *belva!*" (219).

3.8.4d. These animal images are very rarely applied, on the other hand, to men. On one occasion Enrico Lanti is seen "come un *cane allampanato* colla coda attaccata al ventre e l'occhio bramoso intento al tozzo di pane che indovina nella tasca del padrone; e ripeteva il suo ritornello col tono afflitto di un *cane* che ustoli" (229).

3.8.5. It is also in *Storia di una capinera* that Verga presents the reader with a preview of the significant role that nature will come to play in the later works. Here, as Sinicropi correctly notes, nature symbolizes a constant aspiration to a forbidden happiness. [28] The lyrical passages that describe Maria's happiest moments in the midst of nature's beauty become, therefore, highly significant:

> Com'è bella la campagna, Marianna mia! Se tu fossi qui, con me! Se tu potessi vedere codesti monti, al chiaro di luna o al sorger del sole, e le grandi ombre dei boschi, e l'azzurro del cielo, e il verde delle vigne che si nascondono nelle valli e circondano le casette, e quel mare ceruleo, immenso, che luccica laggiù, lontan lontano, e tutti quei villaggi che si arrampicano sul pendio dei monti, che sono grandi e sembrano piccini accanto alla maestà del nostro vecchio Mongibello! Se vedessi com'è bello da vicino il nostro Etna! (...) Tutto qui è bello, l'aria, la luce, il cielo, gli alberi, i monti, le valli, il mare (133-34).

> Quando siamo giunti in cima al monte, che magnifico spettacolo! Il castagneto non arriva sin là, e dalla vetta del monte si può godere la vista di uno sterminato orizzonte. Il sole tramontava da un lato, mentre la luna sorgeva dall'altro: alle due estremità due crepuscoli diversi, le nevi dell'Etna che sembravano di fuoco, qualche nuvoletta trasparente che viaggiava per l'azzurro del firmamento come un fiocco di neve, un profumo di tutte le vigorose vegetazioni della montagna, un silenzio solenne, laggiù il mare che s'inargentava ai primi raggi di luna, e sul lido, come una macchietta biancastra, Catania, e la vasta pianura in

---

[28] "La natura nelle opere di Giovanni Verga," *Italica,* XXXVII-2 (1960), 96 in particular.

> fondo limitata da quella catena di monti azzurri, e solcata
> da quella striscia lucida e serpeggiante che è il Simeto, e
> poi, grado grado salendo verso di noi, tutti quei giardini,
> quelle vigne, quei villaggi che ci mandano da lontano il
> suono dell'avemaria, la vetta superba dell'Etna che si slan-
> cia verso il cielo, e le sue vallate che già sono tutte nere,
> e le sue nevi che risplendono degli ultimi raggi del sole, e
> i suoi boschi che fremono, che mormorano, che si agitano.
> (144-45)

By contrast, they will intensify the mental suffering that she will later experience. It seems, in fact, that nature's role here is quite reminiscent of Leopardi's view of nature as a "matrigna." The faith and hope that nature inspires in Maria prove to be at the end deceptive and painful. Seen in this light, nature begins to acquire that preponderant force and power best to be displayed in *I Malavoglia,* where a natural element such as the sea will dole out life and death indiscriminately and become a degenerating factor in the life of that family.

3.8.6. In conclusion, it is also in *Storia di una capinera* that the first hints of an anthropomorphized nature are noticed. Needless to say, the examples found are feeble especially when compared to the strong force, let us say, of the "brontolone" sea of *I Malavoglia;* but seen within the general picture of Maria's personality and tender affection, they do have a significant validity. In addition to her humane treatment of Vigilante and Carino, a dog and a bird, at times Maria describes nature's elements with human-pertaining terms: "boschi che *fremono,* che *mormorano,* che *si agitano*" (145), "Era un *povero mazzolino* il mio (. . .). Il mio *povero mazzolino* sembrava tutto *vergognoso* accanto a quei fiori *superbi*" (150).

CONCLUSION

In general the foregoing study may be said to have isolated certain defining tendencies in Verga's manipulation of language in his early works. The most general and omnipresent tendency is that of a conscious and rigid excision of the Sicilian element, in conjunction with a complementary and equally conscious attempt to adhere on all linguistic levels both to a general literary norm and, in frequent instances, to a specifically Florentine norm. Furthermore, and more specifically for an understanding of the particular dynamics of this early language usage, the Florentine norm to which Verga adheres preserves consistently in these works a marked tendency toward identification with a Florentine spoken norm. The process of identification, however, reflects the historico-literary situation and is therefore asymptotic.

A closer inspection reveals the following specifics:

PHONOLOGY: The Sicilian element, although tightly controlled in general, is relatively more prevalent on this level than elsewhere. This is evidenced, for example, in the preference for the *a + double* consonant forms in cases where the standard norm would omit the gemination with its preceding vowel (e.g., *addomesticare* and *abbadare* vs. *domesticare* and *badare*) and in the preference for *q* over *c* in certain words.

Most times, however, Verga functions within the limits of a more general literary (and Florentine) norm. Within this norm a preference for new forms coexists with an archaizing tendency. As a result there are frequent hybrid juxtapositions (e.g., oscillation between a given diphthong and its equivalent monophthong; use and omission of the prosthetic *i*, the apheretic *e* and of the oxytonic accent).

MORPHOSYNTAX: Generally Verga adheres to the literary norm and often displays a degree of conservativism in his selection of forms. This is evidenced primarily in his use of certain personal pronouns (*ei, ella, dessa*), in his clear predilection for pronominal enclitic forms, adverbial locutions (*poscia, indi*, et al.), gerundial constructions and both archaic and syncopated inflections of the imperfect indicative.

The Florentine influence, although always within limits, predominates decisively over the Sicilian element. At times, however, the use of the past absolute indicates a Sicilian preference, although the importance of this preference is attenuated by the relative infrequency of its occurrence.

There are also present certain forms which, because of their persistent conspicuousness, may be seen as essentially characteristic of Verga's prose. Included among these are: oscillation in the use of the preposition *di* before such verbs as *tentare, cercare, sperare* and *credere*; the marked preference for conjunctions with *che* and for very frequent similes with *come*; the consistent and emphatic use of anaphoric forms.

LEXICON: The most conspicuous feature of Verga's lexicon is its progressive assimilation to the Florentine spoken norm, an assimilation which heralds the effective subordination of the Sicilian element. This process is best evidenced in the last work of this period, *Eros*.

In his discriminating selection of forms, phrases and themes for the delineation of the Florentine society within his purview, Verga displays distinctive ability. These early works also contain the statement of some themes that were to emerge as central in his later works. The two principal themes are those of the family and animal metaphors.

> L'espressione poetica comincia precisamente là dove la sforzo espressivo in qualche modo si placa ... non che questo sforzo venga mai meno, anzi l'angoscia provata dal poeta nel cercare l'espressione adeguata è uno dei grandi stimoli, talvolta l'oggetto stesso, della sua attività creatrice. Ma il sigillo della poesia pare che stia nell'istante in cui l'artista riesce a staccarsi dalla pena della sua creazione. [1]

---

[1] B. Terracini, *Analisi stilistica*, pp. 53-54.

Verga comes closest to this "espressione poetica" with *I Mala-voglia* and *Mastro-don Gesualdo*, where his poetic intuition is expressed in a language that reflects the highest and most intense moment of the difficult transformation of his native tongue. But for Verga, as for most writers, arriving at this near "idea platonica della lingua" [2] meant years of trying work and experimentation.

On the technical level Verga's assimilation of his expressive modalities to the Florentine norm was complete. However, the use to which he put this newly assimilated language, namely subliminal parody and satire of that same Florentine society, as evidenced most conspicuously in the last of these works, *Eros*, indicates that Verga was beginning to reject spiritually and artistically what he had accepted technically. It is precisely the tension and the dissonance between this modal versatility and spiritual skepticism that suggest that Verga was rejecting that Florentine society as material for his artistic productivity. At least a partial reason for this rejection lies in Verga's judgment that his verbal conformity was the harbinger of a forthcoming conformity of his entire person, spiritual and artistic, to the values of that same society. In view of his exposure of the hypocrisy and in-authenticity [3] of these values in these works, such a conformity could not but be hypocrisy on his part also. Hence, the spiritual and poetic return to Sicily and with it a truly sincere expression. He finally comes to realize that a literary language cannot, contrary to his original belief, be found in any geographic area but only in one's self when he sees it as the internal result — to paraphrase Bally — of an aesthetic need incom-

---

[2] L. Russo, *Verga*, p. 282.

[3] This is the term adopted by Giachery in his *Verga e D'Annunzio* (Milano, 1968), p. 126. He gives this term the same definition given to it by Karl Jaspers in his *Psicologia delle visioni del mondo*, trans. Vincenzo Loriga (Roma, 1950), p. 49. We would like to quote here the definition as it appears in Giachery's book since it seems quite appropriate for the society that Verga is presenting:

> L'inautentico non è una menzogna, nè un inganno consapevole, anzi inganna esso stesso chi lo vive e lo sperimenta di persona, così come inganna il prossimo. Non è privo di realtà, ma di efficacia reale, non è una menzogna ma una mendacità. L'autentico è ciò che è profondo in contrapposizione a ciò che è superficiale: per esempio ciò che tocca il fondo di ogni esperienza psichica di contro a ciò che ne sfiora l'epidermide, ciò che dura di contro a ciò che è momentaneo, ciò che è cresciuto e si è sviluppato con la persona stessa di contro a ciò che la persona ha accattato o imitato. (pp. 126-27)

patible with the banality and above all with the inadequacy of the common norm. [4] No longer is language for him an historical form, "una cosa fatta," [5] but it becomes the consciously arrived at result of the interaction between society and individual creativity. Further, Verga's individual creativity was diffracted through his regional background. His position vis-a-vis the related problems of question of regional language, national norm, and artistic synthesis is well described by Sapir:

> The greatest ... literary ... artists are those who have known subconsciously to fit or trim the deeper intuition to the provincial accents of their daily speech. In them there is no effect of strain, their personal 'intuition' appears as completed synthesis of the absolute art on intuition and the innate, specialized art of the linguistic medium. [6]

Therefore, his stay in Florence, as transient as it may have been, proved to be a very worthwhile experience. It broadened his spectrum of ideas and helped in making him more aware of his needs. It provided him with the tools with which to experiment and his literary results, although "romanzeschi e passionali" [7] in their mood, served as the necessary and autonomous antecedents to the desolate philosophy that was later to be incorporated into his mature works.

[4] See C. Bally, *Traité de stylistique française* (Paris, 1909), I, 237.
[5] L. Russo, *Verga,* p. 281.
[6] E. Sapir, *Language* (New York, 1939), p. 240.
[7] Biondolillo's remarks in "Inchiesta sull'opera del Verga," in *Studi verghiani,* ed. Lina Perroni (Palermo, 1929), p. 50.

SELECTED BIBLIOGRAPHY

PRIMARY SOURCES:

Verga, Giovanni. *Una peccatrice, Storia di una capinera, Eva, Tigre reale.* 3rd ed. Biblioteca Moderna Mondadori. Milano: Mondadori, 1965.
————. *Eros.* 2nd ed. Biblioteca Moderna Mondadori. Milano: Mondadori, 1965.
————. *I Carbonari della montagna.* 4 vols. Catania: Galatola, 1861-62.
————. *Opere.* Edited by Luigi Russo. Milano-Napoli: Ricciardi, 1961.
————. *Tutte le novelle.* 2 vols. 5th ed. Biblioteca Moderna Mondadori. Milano: Mondadori, 1963.

SECONDARY SOURCES:

Ageno, Franca Brambilla. *Il verbo nell'italiano antico.* Milano-Napoli: Ricciardi, 1964.
Ascoli, G. I. "L'Italia dialettale." *Archivio Glottologico Italiano,* VIII (1882-85), 98-128.
————. "Proemio." *Archivio Glottologico Italiano,* I (1873), V, XLI.
Bally, Charles. *Le langage et la vie.* Paris: Payot, 1926.
————. *Linguistique générale et linguistique française.* 3rd ed. Berne: A. Francke, 1950.
————. *Traité de stylistique française,* 1st vol., 2nd ed. Heidelberg: Carl Winters Universitats-Buchhandlung, n.d.
Battaglia, Salvatore and Pernicone, Vincenzo. *La grammatica italiana.* 2nd ed. Torino: Loescher, 1960.
Battisti, Carlo and Alessio, Giovanni. *Dizionario etimologico italiano.* 5 vols. Firenze: Barbèra, 1950-57.
Bergin, Thomas G. *Giovanni Verga.* New Haven: Yale University Press, 1931.
Bertoni, Giulio. *Italia dialettale.* Milano: Hoepli, 1916.
Bloomfield, Leonard. *Language.* New York: Holt, 1933.
Brunot, Ferdinand. *La pensée et la langue: Méthode, principes et plan d'une théorie nouvelle du langage appliquée au français.* 3rd ed. Paris: Masson, 1936.
Bull, William E. *Time, Tense and the Verb.* University of California Publications in Linguistics, Vol. 19. Berkeley: Los Angeles, 1960.

Caccia, Ettore. *Tecniche e valori dal Manzoni al Verga.* Firenze: Olschki, 1969.

Cane, Eleonora. *Il discorso indiretto libero nella narrativa italiana del Novecento.* Roma: Silva, 1969.

Cardini, Massimiliano. "L'*ino* del parlare fiorentino." *Lingua Nostra,* V (1943), 35-38.

Cardona, Giorgio Raimondo. *Linguistica generale.* Roma: Armando Armando, 1969.

Carducci, Giosue. *Prose.* Bologna: Zanichelli, 1924.

Cavallaro, Giovanni. *Dizionario siciliano-italiano.* Acireale: Bonanno, 1964.

Cecchetti, Giovanni. *Leopardi e Verga.* Firenze: La Nuova Italia, 1962.

Chiappelli, Fredi. *Nuovi studi sul linguaggio del Machiavelli.* Firenze: Le Monnier, 1969.

————. *Studi sul linguaggio di Machiavelli.* Firenze: Le Monnier, 1952.

————. "Una lettura verghiana: 'La Lupa'," *Giornale storico della letteratura italiana,* 139 (1962), 370-83.

Cirese, Alberto. "I proverbi nei *Malavoglia.*" In *Pagine di critica letteraria.* Ed. Paolo Acrosso. Vol. III. Palermo: Palumbo, 1963.

Coseriu, Eugenio. *Teoría del lenguaje y lingüística general.* Madrid: Bibiblioteca Románica Hispánica. 1962.

Croce, Benedetto. *La letteratura della nuova Italia.* Vol. III. Bari: Laterza, 1922.

De Gregorio, Giacomo. *Appunti di fonologia siciliana.* Palermo: Amenta, 1886.

————. *Saggio di fonetica siciliana.* Palermo: Amenta, 1890.

De Mauro, Tullio. *Storia linguistica dell'Italia unita.* Universale Laterza, 17. Bari: Laterza, 1965.

D'Ovidio, Francesco and Meyer Lubke. *Grammatica storica della lingua e dei dialetti italiani.* Translated by E. Polcari. 2nd rev. ed. Milano: Hoepli, 1919.

D'Ovidio, Francesco. *Le correzioni ai "Promessi sposi."* Napoli: Guida, 1933.

Degregorio, Ottone. "L'abuso dell'imperfetto." *Lingua Nostra,* VII (1946), 70-71.

Devoto, Giacomo and Altieri, Maria Luisa. *La lingua italiana: storia e problemi attuali.* Edizioni Rai, 172. Torino: Eri, 1968.

Devoto, Giacomo. *Nuovi studi di stilistica.* Firenze: Le Monnier. 1962.

————. *Profilo di storia linguistica italiana.* 4th ed. Firenze: La Nuova Italia, 1966.

Ebneter, Th. "Aviri a + infinitif et le problème du futur en sicilien." *Cahiers Ferdinand de Saussure,* 23 (1966), 33-48.

Fanfani, Pietro. *Vocabolario della pronunzia toscana.* Firenze: Le Monnier, 1879. *

————. *Vocabolario dei sinonimi.* Milano: Di Paolo Carrara, 1865.

————. *Vocabolario dell'uso toscano.* Firenze: Barbèra, 1863.

Ferrari, Aldo. *La preparazione intellettuale del Risorgimento* (1748-1789). Milano: Treves, 1923.

Finzi, Giuseppe. *Grammatica italiana.* Torino: Lattes, 1911.

————. *Regole ed esercizi di grammatica italiana.* 9th ed. Torino: Lattes, 1911.

Fornaciari, Raffaello. *Grammatica italiana dell'uso moderno.* 2nd ed. Firenze: Sansoni, 1882.

Fornaciari, Raffaello. *Sintassi italiana dell'uso moderno.* 2nd ed. Firenze: Sansoni, 1884.
Gabrielli, Aldo. *Dizionario linguistico moderno.* 5th ed. Milano: Mondadori, 1969.
Gentile, Giovanni. *Gino Capponi e la cultura del secolo decimonono.* Rev. 2nd ed. Firenze: Vallecchi, 1926.
Giachery, Emerico. *Verga e D'Annunzio.* Milano: Silva, 1968.
Grandgent, Charles H. *From Latin to Italian: An Historical Outline of the Phonology and Morphology of the Italian Language.* Cambridge: Harvard University Press, 1927.
Greimas, Julien A. *Sémantique structurale: recherche de méthode.* Paris: Larousse, 1966.
Guglielmetti, Marziano. *Struttura e sintassi del romanzo italiano del primo Novecento.* Milano: Silva, 1964.
Guillaume, Gustave. *Temps et verbe.* Paris: Champion, 1929.
Gutia, Ioan. "Sull'uso della preposizione *con* nella prosa italiana contemporanea." *Lingua Nostra,* XIV (1953), 13-19.
Hempel, Wido. *Giovanni Vergas Roman "I Malavoglio" un die Wiederholung als erzählerisches Kunsmittel,* Koln Graz, Bohlan: Verlag, 1959.
Herczeg, Giulio. *Lo stile indiretto libero in italiano.* Firenze: Sansoni, 1963.
————. *Lo stile nominale in italiano.* Firenze: Le Monnier, 1967.
————. "Su alcuni usi del presente." *Lingua Nostra,* XXIII (1962), 104-109.
————. "Un uso particolare della preposizione *con* nella prosa contemporanea." *Lingua Nostra,* XX (1959), 14-17.
Hjelmslev, Louis. *Le langage.* Trans. Michel Olsen. Paris: Les Editions de Minuit, 1966.
Jespersen, Otto. *Analytic Syntax.* Copenhagen: Levin and Munksgaard, 1937.
————. *Essentials of English Grammar.* University, Alabama: University of Alabama Press, 1964.
————. *The Philosophy of Grammar.* New York: Holt and Co., 1924.
Leone, Alfonso. "A proposito degli ausiliari." *Lingua Nostra,* XV (1954), 127-131.
————. "Di alcune carrateristiche dell'italiano di Sicilia." *Lingua Nostra,* XX (1959), 85-93.
Lerch, Eugen. "Das imperfektum als Ausdruck der lebhaften Vorstellung." *Zeitschrift für romanische Philologie,* 42 (1922), 311-331.
Llorach, Emilie A. *Estudios de gramática funcional del español.* Madrid: Editorial Gredos, 1970.
Luperini, Romano. *Pessimismo e verismo in Giovanni Verga.* Padova: Cedam, 1968.
Malagoli, Giuseppe, *Ortoepia e ortografia.* 2nd ed. Milano: Hoepli, 1912.
Manzoni, Alessandro. *Prosa.* Vol. I. Firenze: Salani, 1931.
————. *Scritti linguistici.* Edited by Federico Barbieri. Torino: Società Editrice Internazionale, 1924.
Marouzeau, J. *Lexique de la terminologie linguistique.* Paris: Geuthner, 1933.
Masi, Ernesto. *Il Risorgimento italiano.* Firenze: Sansoni, 1917.
Martinet, André. *Elements of General Linguistics.* Trans. Elisabeth Palmer. Chicago. University of Chicago Press, 1964.
————. *A Functional View of Language.* Oxford: Clarendon Press, 1962.
————. ed. *La linguistique, guide alphabétique.* Paris: Denoël, 1969.
————. *La linguistique synchronique: Études et recherches.* Paris: Presses Universitaires de France, 1965.

Marzot, Giulio. *Preverismo, Verga e la generazione verghiana*. Universale Cappelli. Bologna: Cappelli, 1965.

Meillet, Antoine. *Linguistique historique et linguistique générale*. Paris: Champion, 1921.

Migliorini, Bruno. *Linguistica*. 5th ed. Firenze: Le Monnier, 1968.

――――. *Storia della lingua italiana*. 2nd ed. Firenze: Sansoni, 1960.

Migliorini, Bruno and Leone, Alfonso. *Grammatica italiana e avviamento al comporre*. Firenze: Le Monnier, 1963.

Momigliano, Attilio, ed. *Questioni e correnti di storia letteraria*. Milano: Marzorati, 1965.

Mortillaro, Vincenzo, comp. *Nuovo dizionario siciliano-italiano*. 2 vols. Palermo: Tipografia del giornale letterario, 1838-1844.

――――. *Nuovo dizionario siciliano-italiano*. Rev. ed. Palermo: Lao, 1876.

Mourin, Louis. "Il condizionale passato." *Lingua Nostra*, XVII (1956), 8-15.

――――. "L'imperfetto indicativo." *Lingua Nostra*, XVII (1956), 82-87.

Musumarra, Carmelo. *Verga minore*. Pisa: Nistri-Lischi, 1965.

Natali, Giulio. "Storia del 'non so che'." *Lingua Nostra*, XII (1951), 45-49.

Ojetti, Ugo. *Alla ricerca dei letterati*. Milano: Treves, 1895.

Palazzi, Fernando. *Novissimo dizionario della lingua italiana*. 2nd. ed. Milano: Ceschina, 1964.

Perroni, Lina, ed. *Studi verghiani*. Palermo: Del Sud, 1929.

Petrocchi, Pietro. *Grammatica della lingua italiana*. Milano: Treves, 1909.

Piccito, Giorgio. *L'articolo determinativo in siciliano*. Firenze: Sansoni Antiquariato, 1954.

Raya, Gino. *La lingua di Verga*. Firenze: Le Monnier, 1962.

Rigutini, Giuseppe and Cappuccini, Giulio. *I neologismi buoni e cattivi*. New rev. ed. Firenze: Barbèra, 1926.

Rigutini, Giuseppe and Fanfani, Pietro. *Vocabolario italiano della lingua parlata*. 2nd. ed. Firenze: Barbèra, 1893.

Rohlfs, Gerhard. *Grammatica Storica della lingua italiana e dei suoi dialetti: Fonetica*. Translated by Salvatore Persichino. Piccola Biblioteca Einaudi. Torino: Einaudi, 1966.

――――. *Grammatica storica della lingua italiana e suoi dialetti: Morfologia*. Translated by Temistocle Franceschi. Torino: Einaudi, 1968.

――――. *Grammatica storica della lingua italiana e dei suoi dialetti: Sintassi e formazione delle parole*. Translated by Temistocle Franceschi and Maria Caciagli Fancelli. Torino: Einaudi, 1969.

Ronconi, Alessandro. "L'imperfetto descrittivo." *Lingua Nostra*, V (1943), 90-93.

Rosiello, Luigi. *Struttura, uso e funzione della lingua*. Firenze: Vallecchi, 1967.

Russo, Luisi. *Giovanni Verga*. Universale Laterza. Bari: Laterza, 1966.

Ružička, Otakar. "L'uso dell'ausiliare e la funzione del verbo." *Lingua Nostra*, V (1943), 88-90.

Santangelo, Giorgio. *Storia della critica verghiana*. 2nd ed., 1962; rpt. Firenze: La Nuova Italia, 1967.

Sapir, Edward. *Language: An Introduction to the Study of Speech*. New York: Brace and Co., 1939.

Schick, Carla. *Il linguaggio: natura, struttura, storicità del fatto linguistico*. 3rd ed. Piccola Biblioteca Einaudi. Torino: Einaudi, 1960.

Sechehaye, Albert. *Essai sur la structure logique de la phrase*. Paris: Librairie Ancienne Honoré Champion, 1926.

Sinicropi, Giovanni, "La natura nelle opere di Giovanni Verga." *Italica,* XXXVII-2 (1960), 89-108.

Spitzer, Leo. "L'originalità della narrazione nei *Malavoglia.*" *Belfagor,* XI (Gennaio, 1956), 37-53.

Terracini, Benvenuto. *Analisi stilistica: teoria, storia, problemi.* Milano: Feltrinelli, 1966.

————. *Lingua libera e libertà linguistica.* Torino: Einaudi, 1963.

Tommaseo, Niccolò. *Dizionario dei sinonimi della lingua italiana.* Rev. 5th ed. Napoli: Lubrano, 1866.

Tommaseo, Niccolò and Bellini, Bernardo. *Dizionario della lingua italiana.* 7 vols., 1861; rpt. Torino: Torinese, 1924.

Trabalza, Ciro. *Storia della grammatica italiana.* Milano: Hoepli, 1908.

Trabalza, Ciro and Allodoli, Ettore. *La grammatica degl'italiani.* Firenze: Le Monnier, 1938.

Traina, Antonino. *Nuovo vocabolario siciliano-italiano.* 2nd ed. Palermo: Finocchiaro-Orazio, 1890.

————. *Vocabolarietto delle voci siciliane.* New ed. Palermo: Pedone, 1888.

Treves, Eugenio. ... *Si dice?* ... : *dubbi ed errori di lingua e di grammatica.* Rev. 4th ed. Milano: Ceschina, 1961.

Ullmann, Stephen. *The Principles of Semantics.* 2nd ed. New York: Philosophical Library, 1957.

Vita, Nicola. "Genesi del 'discorso rivissuto' e suo uso nella narrativa italiana." *Cultura Neolatina,* XV (1955), 5-34.

Wartburg, Walther von. *Problems and Methods in Linguistics.* Translated by Joyce M. H. Reid. Oxford: Blackwell, 1969.

Weinrich, Harald. *Estructura y función de los tiempos en el lenguaje.* Translated by Federico Latorre. Madrid: Editorial Gredos, 1968.

INDEX

NORTH CAROLINA STUDIES IN THE
ROMANCE LANGUAGES AND LITERATURES

I.S.B.N. Prefix 0-88438

Recent Titles

THE NOVELS OF MME RICCOBONI, by Joan Hinde Stewart. 1976. (Essays, No. 8). *-008-4.*

FIRE AND ICE: THE POETRY OF XAVIER VILLAURRUTIA, by Merlin H. Forster. 1976. (Essays, No. 11). *-011-4.*

THE THEATER OF ARTHUR ADAMOV, by John J. McCann. 1975. (Essays, No. 13). *-013-0.*

AN ANATOMY OF POESIS: THE PROSE POEMS OF STÉPHANE MALLARMÉ, by Ursula Franklin. 1976. (Essays, No. 16). *-016-5.*

LAS MEMORIAS DE GONZALO FERNÁNDEZ DE OVIEDO, Vols. I and II, by Juan Bautista Avalle-Arce. 1974. (Texts, Textual Studies, and Translations, Nos. 1 and 2). *-401-2; 402-0.*

GIACOMO LEOPARDI: THE WAR OF THE MICE AND THE CRABS, translated, introduced and annotated by Ernesto G. Caserta. 1976. (Texts, Textual Studies, and Translations, No. 4). *-404-7.*

LUIS VÉLEZ DE GUEVARA: A CRITICAL BIBLIOGRAPHY, by Mary G. Hauer. 1975. (Texts, Textual Studies, and Translations, No. 5). *-405-5.*

UN TRÍPTICO DEL PERÚ VIRREINAL: "EL VIRREY AMAT, EL MARQUÉS DE SOTO FLORIDO Y LA PERRICHOLI". EL "DRAMA DE DOS PALANGANAS" Y SU CIRCUNSTANCIA, estudio preliminar, reedición y notas por Guillermo Lohmann Villena. 1976. (Texts, Textual Studies, and Translation, No. 15). *-415-2.*

LOS NARRADORES HISPANOAMERICANOS DE HOY, edited by Juan Bautista Avalle-Arce. 1973. (Symposia, No. 1). *-951-0.*

ESTUDIOS DE LITERATURA HISPANOAMERICANA EN HONOR A JOSÉ J. ARROM, edited by Andrew P. Debicki and Enrique Pupo-Walker. 1975. (Symposia, No. 2). *-952-9.*

MEDIEVAL MANUSCRIPTS AND TEXTUAL CRITICISM, edited by Christopher Kleinhenz. 1976. (Symposia, No. 4). *-954-5.*

SAMUEL BECKETT. THE ART OF RHETORIC, edited by Edouard Morot-Sir, Howard Harper, and Dougald McMillan III. 1976. (Symposia, No. 5). *-955-3.*

DELIE. CONCORDANCE, by Jerry Nash. 1976. 2 Volumes. (No. 174).

FIGURES OF REPETITION IN THE OLD PROVENÇAL LYRIC: A STUDY IN THE STYLE OF THE TROUBADOURS, by Nathaniel B. Smith. 1976. (No. 176). *0-8078-9176-2.*

A CRITICAL EDITION OF LE REGIME TRESUTILE ET TRESPROUFITABLE POUR CONSERVER ET GARDER LA SANTE DU CORPS HUMAIN, by Patricia Willett Cummins. 1977. (No. 177).

THE DRAMA OF SELF IN GUILLAUME APOLLINAIRE'S "ALCOOLS", by Richard Howard Stamelman. 1976. (No. 178). *0-8078-9178-9.*

A CRITICAL EDITION OF "LA PASSION NOSTRE SEIGNEUR" FROM MANUSCRIPT 1131 FROM THE BIBLIOTHEQUE SAINTE-GENEVIEVE, PARIS, by Edward J. Gallagher. 1976. (No. 179). *0-8078-9179-7.*

A QUANTITATIVE AND COMPARATIVE STUDY OF THE VOCALISM OF THE LATIN INSCRIPTIONS OF NORTH AFRICA, BRITAIN, DALMATIA, AND THE BALKANS, by Stephen William Omeltchenko. 1977. (No. 180). *0-8078-9180-0.*

OCTAVIEN DE SAINT-GELAIS "LE SEJOUR D'HONNEUR", edited by Joseph A. James. 1977. (No. 181). *0-8078-9181-9.*

THE LIFE AND WORKS OF LUIS CARLOS LÓPEZ, by Martha S. Bazic. 1977. (No. 183). *0-8078-9183-5.*

When ordering please cite the *ISBN Prefix* plus the last four digits for each title.

Send orders to: University of North Carolina Press
Chapel Hill
North Carolina 27514
U. S. A.